C0-DVU-450

A Visitor's Guide to
SOMERSET AND DORSET

KEY FOR MAPS

Towns - Villages

Motorways

Main Roads

County Boundary

Rivers

Canals

Railways

Lakes/Reservoirs

Museum/Art
Gallery/Centre

Cave

Archaeological Site

Building/
Country Park
Gardens

Castle/Fort

Ecclesiastical
Building

Wildlife Park/Zoo
Sanctuary

Other Place
of Interest

Visitor's Guide Series

This series of guide books gives, in each volume, the details and facts needed to make the most of a holiday in one of the tourist areas of Britain and Europe. Not only does the text describe the countryside, villages, and towns of each region, but there is also valuable information on where to go and what there is to see. Each book includes, where appropriate, stately homes, gardens and museums to visit, nature trails, archaeological sites, sporting events, steam railways, cycling, walking, sailing, fishing, country parks, useful addresses — everything to make your visit more worthwhile.

Other titles already published or planned include:
The Lake District (Revised Edition)
The Peak District
The Chilterns
The Cotswolds
North Wales
The Yorkshire Dales
Cornwall
Devon
The Scottish Borders and Edinburgh
Dordogne (France)
Guernsey, Alderney and Sark

A Visitor's Guide To
SOMERSET AND DORSET

Alan Proctor

British Library Cataloguing
in Publication Data

Proctor, Alan
   A visitor's guide to Somerset & Dorset.
   1. Somerset (England)
   — description and travel — Guide-
   books
   2. Dorset (England)
   Description and travel — Guide-books
   I. Title
   914.23'304857   DA670.D7

The colour illustrations were provided
by: J.A. Robey (Barrington Court,
Cerne Abbas, Cerne Giant, Lyme Regis,
Maiden Castle, Montacute House); the
remainder were taken by the author, as
were all the black and white
illustrations.

© Alan Proctor 1983

ISBN 0 86190 089 8 (hardback)
ISBN 0 86190 088 X (paperback)

All rights reserved. No part of this publication may be reproduced, stored in a
retrieval system, or transmitted in any
form or by any means, electronic, mech-
anical, photocopying, recording or other-
wise, without prior permission of Moorland Publishing Company Ltd.

Typeset by Alacrity Phototype-
setters, Banwell Castle,
Weston-super-mare, Avon
and printed in the UK by
Butler and Tanner Ltd, Frome
for the publishers
Moorland Publishing Co Ltd,
9-11 Station Street, Ashbourne,
Derbyshire, DE6 1DE England.
Telephone: (0335) 44486

Contents

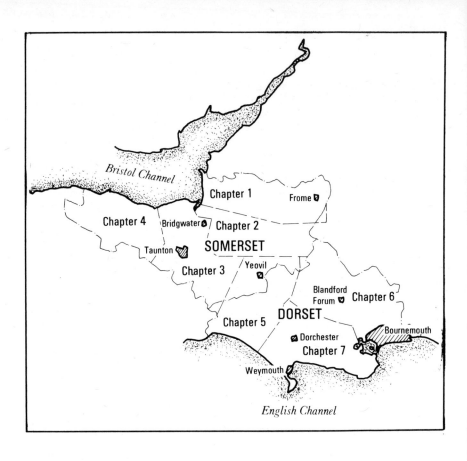

Introduction

The unrivalled scenery of Somerset and Dorset makes these counties ideal holiday areas. Almost every type of setting and scenery can be found here: perfect bays, coves and beaches, world famous showplaces, pretty villages, historic towns and leading holiday resorts. It is no wonder that the area remains top of the list for holidays.

The region has easy access with fast rail and motorway links and there is a wide range of accommodation from the homely farmhouse bed and breakfast to first class hotels. Private apartments, country cottages, chalets, caravan and camping sites, guest houses and moderately priced hotels cater for all tastes.

Somerset is cider country as everybody knows and cider is still made. However the extensive cider apple orchards are only a part of the variations of scenery in this green and pleasant land. In the north the limestone Mendip Hills give way to the sea-level marshes of the 'moors' or levels. Sedgemoor is peaceful and tranquil now, but it has as remarkable a history as any region of Britain. History and legend are difficult to separate; the lines from the hymn "And did those feet in ancient time walk upon Englands mountains green" is based on the supposition that Jesus may have visited here. Joseph of Arimathea, who was a trader and His uncle, is linked to the legend of the Holy Grail which King Arthur and his knights sought. King Alfred burn the cakes at nearby Athelney. The last battle on English soil was fought at Sedgemoor.

Burnham-on-sea and Minehead are two fine resorts on the Bristol Channel coast, while the great landmark of the area is Glastonbury Tor, overlooking the town. There are spectacular caves at Cheddar and Wookey, the great ecclesiastical houses of Wells Cathedral and Glastonbury Abbey, English wines to taste and buy — the list is almost endless. Not long ago, historically speaking, the great lowland areas were awash in winter leaving the higher ground as islands. It was the abbots of Glastonbury who started to drain the area, a process which is still going on, to 'improve' the land. In the nineteenth century steam engines were used for pumping and some are now preserved and open as museums. At high tide the sea outside the walls at Highbridge seems higher than that of the great drains inside! Kings Sedgemoor drain, as it is unromantically called, is a haven for water fowl and fishermen alike.

The heartland of Somerset is the Vale of Taunton Dene. The lush green valley of the River Tone with its fertile meadows and orchards gives way towards the north-east to the Quantock Hills and then to Exmoor. Exmoor is indeed a moor, and much of it is a National Park. The highest point at Dunkery Beacon can be reached quite easily from a nearby, unobtrusive, car park and there are splendid views across the moor. Exmoor has a tiny church at Culbone, a remarkably well preserved clapper bridge at Tarr Steps, and the picturesque villages of Selworthy and Dunster. This is great walking country and tracks over the moor run for many miles. There is plenty of choice whether one wants walking on the high moorland or in the green valleys. The South-west Peninsular Path starts at Minehead and the Severn to Solent Walk starts at Burnham-on-Sea. Exmoor has its own history and traces of this can still be found — from the ancient clapper bridge at Tarr Steps and the Caractacus Stone, a Roman monument, to the still visible traces of nineteenth-century iron ore mining.

Dorset is an unspoilt gem of a county, a rich verdant land. Much of the county is designated an Area of Outstanding Natural Beauty. Inland Dorset has a mixture of lonely heath and fertile valleys, while the north of the county is a pastoral blend of farms woods and river valleys. Ancient tracks abound for the walker, the coast path takes in the whole of the Dorset coastline while inland there is a delightful short walk from Blandford Forum to Bridport known as the Dorset Downs Walk. The Wessex Way enters the county from Wiltshire and runs south to Swanage.

Ancient hill forts abound in the county; Maiden Castle is the largest earthwork in Europe. The nearby county town of Dorchester, founded by the Romans, has a town trail which takes in some of its history. Dorset is Thomas Hardy country and the writer set his scenes in actual places. Jane Austen wrote *Persuasion* while living at Lyme Regis. History is all around still to be seen. The Danes burnt Wareham, while Corfe Castle was a royal prison and the scene of a royal murder.

Shaftesbury once had a great abbey, the remains of which can still be seen, while the steep cobbled Gold Hill is probably the most photographed street in England. The ancient hill figure of Cerne Abbas attracts much speculation and many visitors.

Along the rich coastline, from Bournemouth in the east, the scene could not be more varied with sandy sheltered beaches and charming small resorts. The ever popular Weymouth was a favourite of Charles II. Here there is a sheltered beach a sheltered pleasure craft harbour and a Channel Island rail-boat link. South is Thomas Hardy's 'Gibralter Of Wessex' the Island of Portland. The great sweep of Chesil Beach eventually leads to the cliffs at Lyme Regis, a fossil hunter's paradise. In between is the small harbour of West Bay with Bridport a mile or so inland.

Charming gardens both great and small and historic houses abound in both counties. There are the small quiet houses which must be searched for, where the owners personally conduct small parties, as well as great houses which are among the show places of Britain.

The counties of Somerset and Dorset really do have something for everyone.

1 North Somerset and the Mendips

This chapter deals with northern Somerset and a little of the new county of Avon — green gentle hills in the east and in the west the Mendip Hills with their steep escarpment to the south. To the north the slopes are gentle. To the south the escarpment gives way to the Somerset levels and 'moors'. Not moors in the sense of great heather covered uplands, these are low-lying marshy areas. The name Somerset was derived from an ancient tribe of people who came to the rich verdant areas with their cattle in the summer as summer settlers. In the winter they retreated to the hills as most of the area became waterlogged.

Four main roads go through this area. The A38 near the coast, the A39 from Bath to Wells with the A37 and A367 forming a letter N in the middle joining Midsomer Norton down to Shepton Mallet. Over on the eastern corner the A36 Bath to Salisbury road intercepts the A361 which goes to Frome and then on to Shepton Mallet. From Shepton Mallet the A371 goes to Wells, then along the foot of the Mendip escarpment. Many 'B' roads crisscross the area giving quieter motoring.

The area is steeped in history, going back to the very earliest times, the Romans and the great works of the religious houses (of which there is more in Chapter Two).

The first port of call is the Tropical Bird Gardens at Rode, just off the A36 about four miles north of Frome. In the seventeen acres of garden, which were laid out many years ago, some of the birds fly free. It is a pleasant stroll round the gardens visiting the aviaries which blend well with the surroundings. There are over one thousand birds of almost two hundred different species. A walk through the woods reveals ornamental pheasants and on the string of lakes water birds, including flamingoes and penguins. Children love the pets corner; there is also an aquarium and butterfly and insect exhibition.

A little further south is the village of Beckington, which has some fine gabled and mullioned houses and a fine Norman church tower.

Only a few miles south is the delightful country town of Frome. The modern amenities of the town include bowls, tennis, fishing, a sports centre and an indoor swimming pool. This is a market town built on the steep banks of the River Frome, and near the town shopping centre there is a pleasant modern riverside terrace. Much of the centre of the town is a conservation area; not to be missed are Gentle Street with its old houses, and Cheap Street with the waterway running down the middle. The parish church is built on a site known to have had a Saxon church.

Frome Museum has exhibits and records relating to the town and the nearby villages. Historically, Frome was a woollen town, though this trade has long disappeared. The river in the lower town gave power for the mills and water for the dye houses. In the seventeenth century Judge Jeffreys had twelve men from the town hanged.

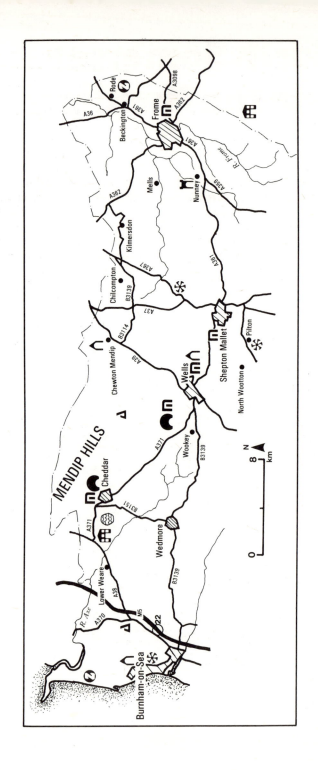

Just over three miles to the east (actually almost a mile inside the Wiltshire border), is Longleat House. Set in magnificent parkland which was landscaped by 'Capability' Brown, this great house is one of the showplaces of the west. Built in 1566 by Sir John Thynne, it contains a very fine collection of French and English furniture, paintings and books. One can picnic in the park and stroll round the Orangery and the lakeside gardens. A five-mile route takes cars through the safari park to see the Lions of Longleat. Obviously there can be no picnics here, but picnics are allowed in the giraffe enclosure. On the islands in the lake live gorillas and chimps, and a boat safari gives a closer view across the lake, in which live hippos and sealions. In what is becoming a tradition with the great show houses there are all the usual attractions of childrens' rides, a miniature railway, Dr Who Exhibition and dolls houses.

Just over a mile north of Frome are the gardens of Orchardleigh Park with a lake and an island church. They are only open on two days in the year, so enquire at the local tourist information office if intending to visit.

Vallis Vale, one mile to the west, is a lovely wooded walk along a deep valley. From Hapsford Mill along Mells River the vale turns south; the northern fork follows a path which

Nunney Castle

leaves the river then rejoins it near Great Elm to continue to Mells, one of the loveliest villages in Somerset. In pre-Reformation times, this was the eastern outpost of Glastonbury Abbey's holdings. The pleasant stone cottages sit among gardens and trees around the splendid sixteenth-century Gothic church with a tower over 100 ft high. It is a three-mile walk back to Frome.

Just over two miles south of Mells lies Nunney, with remains of a fourteenth-century castle. The walls remain, with a cylindrical tower at each corner. A Parliamentary force bombarded the castle in 1645 and forced the Royalist defenders to surrender. The Parliamentarians then stripped the interior. Even the floor boards and joists went and the castle was never inhabited again.

About seven miles north of Frome, by way of the A36 and then east along the A366 towards Trowbridge, is Farleigh Castle. Building started in the late fourteenth century by Sir Thomas Hungerford, whose tomb can be seen in the chapel. Sir Thomas was the first speaker of the House of Commons. The castle replaced an older manor house. The castle chapel was the former village church, but it was incorporated into the castle and a new church was built for the villagers. Now in the care of the Department of the Environment, the castle is sure of preservation.

Along the A366 back south-west to its junction with the A362, and straight across on the B3139 is Kilmersdon. Ammerdown House lies to the right. It is owned by Holiday Fellowship, and is a study centre for short special holidays with a specific purpose. The gardens are open on bank holidays only, and there are attractive walks in

---

Things to do around Frome

Frome
The old town, Gentle Street and Cheap Street, Museum, fishing.

Rode
Tropical Bird Gardens.

Orchardleigh Park
Gardens only, Kilmersdon Church.

Ammerdown Park
Gardens only.

Longleat
Longleat House and Safari Park.

Mells
Walk from Frome to see the village and church.

Nunney
Fourteenth-century moated castle, well preserved remains.

Farleigh Hungerford Castle
Fourteenth-century castle.

---

the extensive grounds.

Kilmersdon is worth a visit for the sake of the church, which dominates the small village and the valley.

The A361 leads towards Shepton Mallet. Some eight miles along at a minor cross road is a left turn to West Cranmore, the home of the East Somerset Railway Museum at Cranmore Railway Station. Here there is a standard gauge railway with its depot and signal box. There are six passenger coaches and seventeen wagons. The steam engine *Green Knight* is here and the star of the show, *Black Prince*, is the largest working steam locomotive in Britain.

Doulting is the next village towards Shepton Mallet and must be mentioned

Market Cross, Shepton Mallet

for its place in history. King Ine of Wessex gave the estate of Doulting to the monastery of Glastonbury in the eighth century. The gift was a memorial to the king's nephew St Aldhelm who died in the village. It was a valuable gift and remained with the abbey until the dissolution. The wealth of Doulting came mainly from great quarries to the north of the village where a creamy white stone was cut. Stone from here was taken to build Wells Cathedral, and was used for work on the abbey at Glastonbury. A great barn was built at the southern end of the village and this is now the main relic of a long Benedictine rule over the rich farmland estate.

Shepton Mallet is mentioned in the Domesday Book and Anglo Saxon records date the origins of the town, but its rise to prosperity was through the weaving trade. As with so many other Somerset towns the weavers originally worked in their own cottages and sent their cloth for finishing to mills along the riverside. The church was built in the fifteenth century and has a fine tower and a splendid wagon roof. Built in 1500 and refurbished in 1841, the market cross is the centrepiece of the shopping area. The jail was built in 1624 and is still a jail, though the buildings in use now are modern; the last execution here was in 1926.

Shepton Mallet is the home of Showerings, the makers of Babycham. From humble beginnings as beer sellers, and later innkeepers, the firm grew to its present size. Myriads of the little bottles of this popular drink go out daily all over the country. Modern amenities in the town include bowls, tennis and an outdoor swimming pool. There is an eighteen-hole golf course just over a mile north of the town off the A37 Bristol road. A cinema also does duty as a theatre, and early closing day is Wednesday.

At the village of Oakhill, almost opposite the golf course, is the Oakhill Manor World of Models. Set high on

---

Things to do around Shepton Mallet

East Somerset Railway
Steam trains.

Oakhill Manor
World of models.

Shepton Mallet
Museum, cinema/theatre, swimming pool, bowls, tennis, horse riding, eighteen-hole golf course, arts and cultural centre.

Vineyards
At Pilton and Wootton.

13

the Mendips the lovely setting for the manor house is a forty-five acre estate, with eight acres of landscaped gardens. Inside the furnished manor house there is a model railway and one of the world's finest collections of land, sea and air transport. In the grounds it is possible to follow the scenic route of the miniature railway on foot, or to ride this fine railway which is hauled by a steam engine at weekends and school holidays.

Almost two miles south, just off the A361, is the village of Pilton. At Pilton Manor Vineyard visitors can take a leisurely stroll and taste the wines. Across the main road and only a little over a mile away at North Wootton are Wootton Vines, another winery, where white wine and cider wine are made in traditional ways. Again visitors are welcome to walk in the vineyard. Geographically both these two villages are on the southern slopes of Mendip, giving the mild protected environment that the vines need. Vines were brought to England by the Romans, but it is only in recent years that the art has been seriously revived.

Wells can easily be reached from North Wootton by either of the roads going in a northerly direction. As Somerset's only cathedral city, Wells attracts many visitors; there is plenty to see in the city and around the area nearby.

Modern amenities are tennis, bowls, a heated open air swimming pool and a nine-hole golf course. There is a theatre in town, and on the eastern outskirts a three-mile nature trail starts from the market square; a guide leaflet is available from the curator of the museum. Blagdon Lake and Chew Valley Lake (both stocked with trout), are about ten miles from Wells in delightful scenery on the Mendip Hills. The panoramic view from the Pen Hill, near the television transmitter, takes in the fringes of Salisbury Plain to the east, while swinging westward the start of the Somerset marshes can be followed to the higher point of Glastonbury Tor. Far away to the west, if the light is right, there may be a glimmer of the sea at Bridgwater Bay. There is a nature trail at Pen Hill starting from near the transmitter, about $2\frac{1}{2}$ miles long and with geological interest as well as plants and birds; a guide is available from the museum.

Regular walks are organized in the area, and the local information office will give details of the variable programmes. Visitors are always welcomed on the walks which are organised in many areas, often by the local branch of the Ramblers' Association. In the case of Wells, the Mendip Society organises regular walks in different areas of Mendip.

Lovers of history and historic buildings will find Wells a most beautiful cathedral city and a veritable treasure trove. The ubiquitous Romans seem to have bypassed Wells and King Ine of the West Saxons has first claim in the record books. He decided to build a church at this point where numerous springs rose from below the Mendips, hence the name of Wells. The cathedral dates from the twelfth century, but much extension and addition went on at least until the fifteenth century. There is much interesting glass in the cathedral dating from the fourteenth century. Over the High Altar the great east window is probably one of the finest of its kind in Britain. The great clock has an inner and outer dial showing the minutes and hours respectively. Phases of the moon are shown and at each quarter hour a tournament of knights takes place. The great clock

The Cathedral, Wells

was made about 1380, possibly at Glastonbury Abbey.

A unique picture is formed by the moated and fortified bishop's palace, one of the oldest inhabited houses in England. In the grounds are the famous springs from which Wells is named. The fortifications were added in the fourteenth century, the main buildings being a little older, when there were some differences of opinion with the townspeople. Though never actually needed at that time, the drawbridge was drawn up in 1831 when Reform Act rioters attacked the Bishop's Palace at Bristol.

Near the bridge, hanging low over the water just below a window, is a bell. The swans living on the moat ring the bell to call for food. This practice is supposed to date back to Victorian times, but a piece of old glass at Nailsea Court seems to suggest that the birds have been doing this little trick for much longer, possibly a few hundred years.

Among other interesting features of the city are the Bishop's Barn, dating from the fifteenth century, and St Cuthbert's Church, said to be the largest parish church in Somerset. Visitors approaching from Cheddar have been known to mistake this church for the cathedral. Llewellyn's Almshouses and the Old Deanery should also be seen along with the Chain Gate, Chapter House, Vicars

---

Things to do in Wells

In the city: museum, cinema and theatre, bowls, tennis, swimming pool and nine-hole golf course. Wells Cathedral, Bishop's Palace. Many medieval buildings both ecclesiastical and secular. Walks and nature trails.

15

Close, the Old Almshouses and Penniless Porch, where beggars used to gather to accost visitors to the cathedral.

The Cathedral Library, built about 1425, is partly open and treasures, manuscripts and books are on display. Wells Museum includes a collection of early Iron Age artifacts excavated from Wookey Hole Cave, as well as pottery from various other Mendip caves. In one of the rooms is a fine collection of coins, minerals and local bird and animal life. There is an abundance of folk relics and a good collection of samplers.

Places of Interest on the Mendips

Wookey Hole
Caves, museum, paper mill, fairground collection, Madame Tussaud's Storeroom. Ebbor Gorge and nature trail, the Moors Nature Trail.

Priddy
An old sheep village high on the Mendips.

Chewton Mendip
The church of St Mary Magdalene.

Burrington
Burrington Combe.

Cheddar
Caves, Museum, Jacob's Ladder, Cheddar Gorge, Nature Trail.

Axbridge
King John's Hunting Lodge, Church, Ambleside Water Gardens, walk near the reservoir.

Nature Trails
Descriptive leaflets from Wells Museum

A pleasant short walk starts from Moat Walk. At the end of the Walk go over a stile, cross the road to a wood and follow the winding walk to the summit of Tor Hill, from where there is a charming view of the cathedral's east side.

There are many interesting houses and odd corners in the city that wait to be discovered, especially the sixteenth-century Crown Hotel and the fourteenth-century bakery in St Thomas Street. New Street is now a respectable area, but once it was the haunt of Mendip miners when they came to town.

Wells is a good place from which to explore Mendip; being a 'tourist' city there is plenty of accommodation, yet it is small enough not to have any traffic problems.

Man has been around Mendip for centuries. A skeleton of a Paleolithic man 12,000 years old was found in the Cheddar caves; his hunting ground was probably on Mendip.

Lead mines were being worked on Mendip before the Roman invasion. Fishermen down on the lower ground used lead weights. The Romans must have known about the lead mines and indeed it has been speculated that they were one of the reasons for their invasion of Britain. Only six years elapsed between the first landing and the full operation of the mines. Two pigs of lead have been found stamped with a name, enabling accurate dating. Charterhouse was the centre of mining for the Romans. Silver was also found and some British states had a silver coinage. Some of the lead no doubt went to Bath where lead pipes still carry water to and from the Roman Baths.

There is ample evidence that the Saxons used lead for church roofs, but there is no further evidence for the working of the mines until the twelfth century when the Bishop of Bath was granted a mining charter by Richard I. Mining went on through the Middle Ages, right up till the first half of the nineteenth century. However by the end of the seventeenth century, the easily accessible deposits had been worked out, the miners had to go deeper and often ran into trouble with flooding.

Other minerals, such as ores of zinc, manganese and iron, were also mined as early as the thirteenth century. Very little is known about the life the miners led. Among the first to record details of the miners' lives were Hannah More and her sister Martha. Hannah devoted herself to improving the lot of the poor. The miners were recorded as having been 'savage, depraved, brutal and ferocious'. No policeman would dare to attempt to arrest a Shipham man, as he would have feared for his life.

The core of the Mendips is carboniferous limestone, a rock that dissolves easily in the small amount of carbonic acid in rainwater. Water either seeping down or welling up chooses the weaker spots, seeping into the cracks which become fissures, which in turn become channels and caves, and eventually the glorious caverns at Wookey Hole and Cheddar.

The surface plateau, in medieval times, was a Royal Forest in the sense that it was a hunting ground or chase. On the site of an ancient Saxon hunting lodge at Axbridge there is a house dating from the sixteenth century, named King John's Hunting Lodge. It is now a National Trust property and is open as a museum.

Monks of the Carthusian order, who

King John's Hunting Lodge. Axbridge Museum

gave Charterhouse its name, developed sheep farming and the wool trade — though goats are recorded in the Domesday Book, fifty goats at Chewton Mendip and sixty-eight at Rodney Stoke. In times of necessity, such as World War II, arable farming was substituted and barley and potatoes were grown. When that necessity receded the farmers went back to sheep, for arable farming is a little precarious on the misty, wind- and rain-swept heights.

Priddy, with its stone circles and barrows, retains the atmosphere of the sheep farming community. There is a stack of hurdles reputed to have stood on the green for three hundred years. Priddy Sheep Fair has been an annual event for many years where the traditions of sheep buying and selling and hiring of staff take place. The Fair still takes place on 18th August every year.

The nearest place to Wells is Wookey Hole, two miles away, where visitors can see the Great Cave with its different chambers and the legend of the Witch of Wookey. There is a paper mill with an exhibition about handmade paper, and an exhibition of fairground figures. A museum houses archaeological finds from the caves and also Madame Tussaud's Store Room. About a mile to the north-west of the village is the Ebbor Gorge national nature reserve. Starting from the car park at Deer Leap Road there are two trails. The shortest is ½ mile long, passing through quiet woodland. The second trail is 1½ miles and is a more strenuous walk passing through a rugged gorge and grassland. Another trail, the Moors Trail, starts from Easton village by the church, just off the Wells to Cheddar road. This trail runs for four miles, and a leaflet is available from Wells Museum. The

Cheddar Gorge

trail traverses a typical section of Somerset level or moor.

Following the A371 north-west leads to Cheddar, famous for giving its name to Cheddar cheese. William Camden, writing in the sixteenth century, said that 'it was famous for the excellent and prodigious great cheeses made there'. Nowadays, of course, Cheddar cheeses may come from New Zealand, but should these not properly be labelled Cheddar *type* cheese? Daniel Defoe wrote in 1722 'The whole village were cow keepers'. Cheddar is now almost as famous for its strawberries as for its caves. The sloping fields between the main road and the hills are well sheltered from the cold north wind and early vegetables as well as strawberries are grown in profusion.

The primitive Celtic belief that some hills were filled with passages in an underground fairy world is understandable after a visit to the Cheddar caves. The glistening colourful rocks often give dramatic effects, and the delicate shading is not caused by the lighting, but by the various minerals in those rocks. Formations have been given names, delightfully descriptive, such as Fairy Grotto, Frozen River and many more. The caves were used as human habitation for many years. In the museum there is a life-size display of Paleolithic man. This first recorded use of the caves dates from 10,000 years ago. In the Dark Ages the caves were used as a refuge by the Romano-British during the fifth and sixth centuries. Many Roman coins, along with weapons and domestic articles, have been found.

These caverns are still not fully explored and most weekends will see the cavers in action. Many caving clubs operate in the region, exploring and searching for new routes. However, the Mendip Rescue Organization does not exist for nothing. Deaths have occurred in the caves, mostly inexperienced amateurs without proper equipment, or people who are trapped by rising waters. Sudden flooding is just one of the hazards, for a summer storm may cause the waters to rise rapidly. So be warned, if you wish to go caving join a club and get expert advice and help. Caves open to the public are, of course, perfectly safe.

The two main caves at Cheddar, Gough's and Cox's, were discovered in the nineteenth century. Cox was a miller digging at the rockface to make room for a new shed when he found his cave. Though Gough's cave was known earlier, Mr Gough and his sons did a tremendous amount of work in making the passages safe for visitors. One may now stroll on smooth paths, conducted by a knowledgeable guide,

without even getting dirty shoes.

For a breathtaking view (and a breathtaking climb) take the 322 steps of Jacob's Ladder up the side of the gorge. The splendid view of the Somerset moors, to the Quantocks and Exmoor, makes the climb well worth the effort. A whole day can easily be spent in the gorge, with Jacob's Ladder, the caves, refreshments, or a full meal in one of the restaurants, as well as the exhibition and museum. The gorge is also the starting point for many walks with some delightful picnicking spots. One may even be able to watch some of the many rock climbers on Cheddar Cliffs. In some places the walls of the gorge rise nearly 500 ft.

Higher up the gorge is the Black Rock Nature Trail. The start is about 1½ miles north of Cheddar, up the gorge, in Black Rock Drive. It is 2 miles long and is a woodland walk with good views over the Mendip countryside.

Charterhouse, two miles north-east from Cheddar, was the chief Roman lead mining area and many Roman coins have been found in the area. Traces of the workings remain in the fields. From the minor road just north of the church, a bridleway leads up to Mendip's highest point — Beacon Batch on Black Down is 325 metres (1,067 ft) high with splendid views and is only slightly lower than the highest point of the Cotswolds. It is possible to walk on down to Cheddar, or to turn north and go down to Burrington Combe.

The deep cut Burrington Combe carries the B3134 down off the plateau to join the A368. Although it is not as spectacular or as deep as Cheddar Gorge, it has its place in history. It was in the combe in 1762 that the Rev Augustus Toplady, a curate of Blagdon, took advantage of a cleft in the rocks to shelter from a storm. While sheltering here he got the idea for his hymn 'Rock of Ages' and a carved inscription records the fact.

Lovers of churches should visit St Mary Magdalene at Chewton Mendip, and Axbridge church. Chewton Mendip church, which is fifteenth century, has one of those splendid towers, Axbridge has some good glass and brasses. Also in Axbridge is the National Trust property known as King John's Hunting Lodge. The house was built about 1500 and is an example of the rising prosperity of the merchants of the times. It is now a museum with changing exhibits. This small village was struck by tragedy in 1973 when a party of women on a day trip to Switzerland were in a plane crash, with great loss of life.

From the church at Axbridge there is a walk south-east to the reservoir. Join a track and turn right; cross the River Yeo and go downstream to recross at the first bridge and head back to the church, about 3½ miles for the round trip.

On the A38, a mile south west from Axbridge, is Lower Weare and the Ambleside Water Gardens and Aviaries. A further three miles along the A38, and just after crossing the M5, is a minor road to East Brent. Brent Knoll was almost certainly an island long ago, before the levels were drained. It rises to 137 metres (450 ft) and is topped by an Iron Age hill fort; it is a conspicuous landmark from miles around and can be seen from South Wales. There is a footpath to the top from a point close to East Brent church.

The villages of Brent Knoll, or South Brent and East Brent, both have churches with interesting features. On the south-western slopes of the hill the church of Brent Knoll has an interest-

Brean Down from Brean Sands

Things to do near the Coast

Brent Knoll
The churches of East Brent and
Brent Knoll. Brent Knoll, walk up
to the hill fort.

Brean Down
Nature reserve on Brean Down.
Tropical Bird Gardens. Sandy
beach.

Burnham on Sea
Eighteen-hole championship golf
course by the sea. Medieval church.
Indoor swimming pool. Tennis.
Bowls. Fishing. Walk along the
river to the old docks at Highbridge.

ing series of bench ends, which tell the
story of a parish priest of long ago
who had a quarrel with the Abbot of
Glastonbury. Both villages were part of
the ecclesiastical estates, and surprisingly the parish priest won. The
carvings commemorate the victory: the
Abbot is shown as a fox and the
parishioners as various animals including geese. In the final cartoon the
Abbot is hanged by the geese. East
Brent church has a fine plaster ceiling
dating from the early part of the
seventeenth century. There are also
some carved bench ends in the nave,
including the arms of the abbey as well
as the initials of Abbot Selwood.

Brent Knoll is only a few miles from
the sea and the road north through
Berrow passes camping and caravan
sites and access points to Brean sands.
At the far end rises Brean Down. This
is really an outcrop of the Mendips
and gives a fine clifftop walk of a mile
or so with exhilarating sea breezes and
wide views. The top is springy turf and
the whole of the Down is a National
Trust property and a nature reserve.

There is a tropical bird garden near
Brean with many exotic birds on show.

South of Berrow is Burnham on Sea,
which has developed from a centre of
early agricultural improvement to a
resort and spa. The town also had a
place in railway and shipping development. Burnham's only medieval relic is
the church; the west tower leans, no
doubt due to the shifting sands below.
A fine Jacobean pulpit and a Georgian
chandelier, the latter made by a brass
founder of Bridgwater named Bayley,
are among its features. The sculptures
now at Burnham once formed part of
the Baroque altarpiece of the Gothic
Chapel at Whitehall Palace.

A curate of the parish, the Reverend
David Davies, helped the advance of
Burnham on Sea by digging wells from
which he hoped to get waters similar to
those discovered at Cheltenham. Both
saline-chalybeate and sulphureous
waters were found; they met with a
mixed reception but the birth of the
town as a resort was assured.

The Reverend Davies was also in-
terested in lighthouses. Burnham overlooks the once busy sea approaches to
Bridgwater and Highbridge. The enter-
prising curate built a new lighthouse
and secured an Act of Parliament
under which he could levy tolls on
passing ships. Trinity House later took
over the sea lanes and in 1832 a new
lighthouse was built.

Modern facilities include an eighteen-
hole golf course, where the West of
England Open Championship is held;
it lies to the north of the town between
Berrow and the sea. Burnham has an
indoor swimming pool and the usual
facilities for bowls, tennis, boating and
fishing.

A walk along the Esplanade leads to
Highbridge, which was once a busy
port. The bridge that gave the town its

East Somerset Railway

name was in reality a dam. At high tides the water on the seaward side was higher than the fresh water of the river. The heyday of the port was in the eighteenth and nineteenth centuries. Movement of goods was greatly helped by the Glastonbury Canal which opened in 1833. Railways superseded the canal in 1854, backed by the shoemakers Clarks of Street, who wanted better transport for their growing business.

The Somerset and Dorset Railway (the old S and D was affectionately known as 'slow and dirty') repaired engines at Highbridge well into this century. Local business interests helped the docks to expand, they even survived the withdrawal of the railway interest in the 1930s. Right up to 1948 the port remained working as a coastal port, but although it is now almost derelict it is still interesting.

2 Central Somerset

From the eastern part of the county where the gentle hills roll down from Wiltshire the land drops down to the Somerset levels or moors. The levels are divided roughly by the Polden Hills. From Shepton Mallet the A361 goes to Glastonbury and on to Taunton. Coming from Wells the A39 goes through to Bridgwater. Both these routes follow what high ground there is and from Glastonbury to Bridgwater the A39 runs along the top of the Poldens. In the old days the levels in winter were often flooded and large shallow lakes appeared. Any travelling had to be along higher ground. The monks of Glastonbury were largely responsible for the countryside looking

as it is now, when they started draining the moors.

As in Chapter One we are going to take in a little bit of Wiltshire, as it seems a shame to be so close to such lovely places without visiting them. This time it is a famous Wiltshire beauty spot, Stourhead Gardens. The house and grounds are owned by the National Trust and the house has a collection of works of art, and furniture by Thomas Chippendale. Included in the 2,500-acre estate is White Sheet Down which has a neolithic enclosure and White Sheet Castle, an Iron Age hill fort. The whole estate includes the villages of Stourton and Kilmington, and there

The Somerset Levels

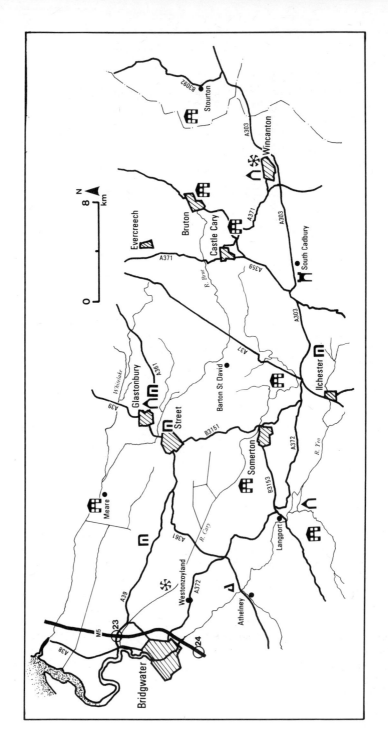

Alfred's Tower

are 300 acres of woodland. Through the woods to the west beyond the lakes there are footpaths up to Alfred's Tower, and a round trip from the village is about 6 miles. The house was built in 1721 and the gardens laid out in 1741. Famous for their beauty, they are among the finest examples of landscape design of this period. Round the lakes and through the lower woodlands are some of the best examples of conifers, beech and rhododendrons in the country, and there are many rarities.

Across the B3092 from Stourhead the walk up to White Sheet Down, which is about 4 miles for the round trip, gives splendid views south to Shaftesbury and the River Stour valley as it winds southwards through Dorset. There is a picnic site on the estate near Alfred's Tower. At the Spread Eagle Inn near the entrance to the gardens refreshments are available, from morning coffee to tea and dinner. For local fishing enquire at the office at the garden's entrance.

Driving south on the B3092 and a west turn on the A303, leads to Wincanton. The town itself is fortunately by-passed, so is fairly quiet. It is a thriving market town surrounded by rich pastureland, and has some interesting buildings. It is almost exactly

Places of interest near Wincanton

Stourhead House and Gardens
Elegant Palladian house and beautiful landscaped gardens. The house contains some original furniture. Built in 1722 by Colen Campbell, the gardens landscaped by Henry Hoare. Nearby White Sheet Hill.

Bruton
National Trust, sixteenth-century dovecote a half mile south and over the railway. Church of interest.

Cadbury Castle
A major hill fort with much use down through the ages. Possibly the Camelot of King Arthur.

Castle Cary
Hadspen House gardens. Lockup, small museum.

Wincanton
Parish church of interest. Redlynch Lake to the north has good fishing. Interesting historic town.

midway between London and Plymouth, at one time it was a re-mount point for couriers and later became an important staging post for coaches on their way to and from the west. As many as seventeen coaches a day stopped in the coaching heyday.

The parish church dates from the fourteenth century, but was rebuilt in 1889. There is a medieval carving of St Eligius in the north porch, while in the churchyard is a monument to Nathaniel Ireson, one of the town's most notable men, who had a hand in much local building.

From the village of Cucklington, about three miles south-east, there is a fine ridge walk of a mile, north from the church, giving good views over the surrounding countryside. From the local tourist information office a leaflet can be obtained giving directions for a circular 'Wincanton Walk' about 3 miles long.

South Cadbury Church

26

On the way north from Wincanton on the B3081 towards Bruton is Redlynch Lake, set in superb countryside and with some very good fishing. Seven-pound carp and four-pound tench can be taken. Check with the information office in Wincanton for a phone number for enquiries.

Bruton is a small town, but like so much of this area it has its place in history. Berkeley Square in London is named after the first Baron Berkeley who invested in what was then open land. The Baron's home town is also commemorated in London by Bruton Street. When Henry VIII dissolved the monasteries one of the lucky Somerset families were the Berkeleys. The king's standard bearer at that time was Sir Maurice Berkeley, and he was given the abbey at Bruton and its lands. The first baron was ennobled for his services to the Royalist cause during the Civil War. Tombs of the Berkeley family can be seen in Bruton church.

The town had one of the first fulling mills in England, built about 1290. Another famous son of the town, who started life as a stable boy was Hugh Sexey, who made good and eventually founded the famous Sexey's School.

Bruton is one of the gems of the quiet Somerset country — the splendid Gothic parish church, the almshouses, the pack horse bridge and the dovecote make this historic small town well worth a visit. The dovecote is National Trust and is a sixteenth-century roofless type standing about ½ mile south of the town centre.

Down the A359 about 4 miles southwest is Hadspen House, where the ornamental gardens are open. A turn up the A371 leads to Castle Cary. The best surviving feature here is the old lockup which was built in 1779 and is only 7 ft in diameter. It has a pagoda-like roof. There is a small museum in the town which is worth visiting, open every weekday from April to October.

South from Castle Cary is South Cadbury and Cadbury Castle, and is a claimant to the title of Camelot — and probably a stronger one than the Cornish claim for Arthur's last battle. The wounded Arthur was taken to Glastonbury, a long way from Cornwall, but only fifteen miles from Cadbury and at one time joined to it by a track. After Arthur's death Queen Guinevere took holy vows and later became Abbess of Amesbury. When she eventually died Lancelot took her body to Glastonbury, the Avalon of legend, and she was buried beside Arthur.

The hill fort is certainly one of the greatest of the hill forts of southern Britain. A walk round the mighty ramparts is almost a mile.

Traces of Neolithic, Bronze Age and Iron Age use have been found by archeologists at Cadbury Castle. After the Roman legions departed it was refortified and used by the Romano-

---

Places to visit around Somerton

Lytes Cary
National Trust, a manor house with a fourteenth-century chapel and fifteenth-century great hall.

Fleet Air Arm Museum
Near Ilchester. The history of the Fleet Air Arm since its early days. More than forty historic aircraft are on display, Concorde 002 is also housed here.

Somerton
A quiet town, medieval market cross. Thatchcap Windmill at High Ham, National Trust, a thatched windmill dating from 1820.

Market, Somerton

British. This was about AD 500, possibly its Arthurian period. Later, about AD 1000, it was again refortified by Ethelred the Unready for defence against the Danes. A mint was established here and much of the coinage was used to pay off the Danes (Danegeld as it was called). Most of the surviving Cadbury coins now lie in Scandinavian museums. The views from the walk round the ramparts reveal the scope of this place as a defensive site, movements to the north and west would have been spotted in plenty of time to get organised. The important route of the Fosse Way is clearly visible.

Only 6 miles along the main A303 is the Fleet Air Arm Museum at Yeovilton. The museum is open all year, daily, and shows the early development of naval flying from its origins in 1910 to the present. Concorde 002 is also on display and a visit will take up most of the day.

Just north of the Fleet Air Arm Museum, a little way up the minor road to Charlton Mackerell, is Lytes Cary, a property of the National Trust. This typical Somerset manor house was the home of the Lyte Family for five hundred years. The great hall is fifteenth century with later additions including the sixteenth-century great

Places of interest around Langport

Abbey Ruins, Muchelney
Just over a mile south of Muchelney, easily reached by riverside path.

Midelney Manor
Drayton. A sixteenth-century manor house. Falconry mews, heronry and gardens.

Langport
The church is of interest. Hanging Chapel, once part of the town gate, dating from 1353. Riverside walks.

Somerton Church

chamber. There is a fourteenth-century chapel. Probably the best known member of the Lyte family was the Elizabethan Sir Henry Lyte, who wrote what for those days, and long after, was the standard work on horticulture. The gardens date from that time.

Almost opposite the drive to Lytes Cary is a minor road to Kingsdon, a quiet village with a nice fifteenth-century church right in among the cottages. The church houses the stone figure of a knight who ruled Kingsdon in the thirteenth century when Edward III was king.

Somerton is just under 3 miles along the B3151. Somerton was once an important town, not only to Somerset but to all of Wessex. To its good fortune it has been by-passed by the modern world. Here is the delightful Broad Street, the old town hall, some excellent Georgian houses and a medieval market cross built during the

reign of Charles II. It was a royal manor and a castle superseded the original Saxon fort. The castle does not appear to have been used as a castle after the reign of Henry III, but was probably used as a jail. It is believed that the White Hart inn covers part of the site. The church, which is near the market cross, has a transeptal southern tower. Royal control must have been the key to the long survival of what is now a delightful little town.

Anyone wanting an energetic walk can start from Somerton and walk north to Etsome Farm, then cross the River Cary. Keep going north by a track, then a footpath to Dundon. Take the footpath round Dundon Hill with extensive views over the surrounding moors and hills. From Hayes Farm go south to join a minor road and so back to Somerton, about 7 miles round.

Alternatively from Dundon keep

going north to cross another stretch of moor and pass Ivy Thorn Manor to climb up Ivy Thorn Hill near the Youth Hostel. Turn left by the road, which for most of the way is unfenced so that it is possible to walk through the trees. Continue to Walton Hill and turn left on a footpath just past the windmill. Near the bottom of the hill meet the road at the top of a T-junction. Go south-west down the road for $\frac{1}{4}$ mile and straight on down a track where the road goes right. Cross Eighteen Feet Rhyne and cross Somerton Moor, then join and follow the minor road back to Somerton. This is a round trip of about 14 miles. Ivy Thorn Hill and Walton Hill are National Trust properties, the total area being just under 90 acres, and there are some good viewpoints from here to both sides of the hills.

Just to the east is the village of Butleigh, which was the home of the Hood family. On the great hill nearby is the Hood monument. Admiral Hood died in 1814, and the towering column was erected by his officers to his memory.

West of Somerton a minor road branches off the B3153 just on the town outskirts on a minor road to High Ham where there is a thatched windmill. It now belongs to the National Trust and dates from 1820; it was working until 1910.

High Ham is on a rocky peninsula looking over the moors to the north, while a narrow pass to the south is guarded by Langport. The River Parrett passes through this gap on its way to Bridgwater. The other side of Langport is a long narrow peninsula with Curry Rivel at its north-western end. Over these long extensions of the moors meander the Rivers Yeo, or Ivel, and Isle to join the Parrett at Lang-

port, and then only a few miles downstream the River Tone joins near Burrow Bridge.

A study of detailed maps of the area shows that the lower-lying areas such as the wide stream valleys south of Langport, and West Sedge Moor, northwest of Curry Rivel, have no buildings. This is further evidence of the floods of years ago, there was little point in building a barn if the food stored in it was ruined by winter floods. So all the buildings were built on the higher ground. Much of West Sedge Moor even here, fifteen miles from the sea, is only 5m (16ft) above sea level. The River Parrett near Langport is about the same level, so the rivers are sluggish and slow to drain the surrounding land.

A mile or so south of Langport are the ruins of Muchelney Abbey. The abbey was founded in 939 by the Benedictines and was an important ecclesiastical establishment, though not

---

Places of Interest on the Moors

Burrow Mump
An ancient hill site with an unfinished chapel on the summit.

Burrowbridge/Allermoor Pumping Station
Steam engines and pumps on display.

Westonzoyland
Nearby site of the Battle of Sedgemoor in 1685. Prisoners were brought to the parish church. Also pumping station nearby with a steam pump and other interesting items.

Polden Hills
On the way to Street, viewpoints over the moors.

The Hanging Chapel, Langport

as large as Glastonbury. During the dissolution Muchelney Abbey escaped immediate destruction, but gradually sank into decay. The Priest's House survives and is owned by the National Trust, but is not generally open to the public except by written appointment. In the tiny village the church and cottages contain some pieces salvaged from the abbey.

West across the River Parrett is the village of Drayton, and Midelney Manor. The sixteenth-century manor house was once part of the abbey estates and since the dissolution has been the property of the Trevilian family. There are the very interesting falconer's mews to be seen, as well as

the gardens and a heronry.

Curry Rivel is under a mile away and straddles the A378. A recommended walk is west from the church along a minor road, which soon turns north. At a T-junction go straight ahead on a track, take the first left and at the end of the track go north to the woods, then swing left in a large loop to the road at Heale and so back to the start. This 2-mile walk has good views over West Sedge Moor from near the summit of Red Hill.

Langport church is worth visiting; there is some find stained glass and among the saints depicted is Joseph of Arimathea. The Hanging Chapel has no connection with Judge Jeffreys's rampage through the west country as might be supposed. The term hanging refers to the fact that it once perched on top of the town gate and now seems to hang in the air. It was built in 1353 and the chapel served as a merchant guild before having a spell as town hall.

Langport has been identified by scholars as Llongborth, and if this is correct then the town existed in the sixth century. There is a reference, in an ancient Welsh book, to a battle fought here by Geraint in the time of King Arthur. Geraint was king of the Dumnonii, the tribe occupying the area before the Roman invasion. The town was important enough to have had a mint for a long time. The fact that the River Parrett could be forded here made it an ideal place for a town. In the thirteenth century an imposing stone bridge with nine arches, and called Great Bow, was built here. All the houses in Bow Street lean backwards, the fronts having better foundations than the back. The great bridge was pulled down in 1840 to make way for river traffic at a period when Langport had some prosperity as a port. River traffic took goods to Ilchester and Yeovil.

There are some good riverside walks along the river banks from Langport. One suggested route is east from Langport along the north bank. Change sides at the first bridge and go south to Muchelney to view the abbey ruins before walking back again, to make a four mile round trip.

From Langport a minor road leads to Burrow Bridge and the Allermoor Pumping Station, one of the stations which helped keep the moors drained. Among the exhibits are three huge steam engines and pumps built by Easton and Amos in the 1860s. Nearby

Places of interest in and around Glastonbury

Abbey Ruins
King Arthur's burial place.

The Tor
Splendid views from the top.

Abbey Barn
The home of the Somerset Rural Life Museum.

The Tribunal
Lake village museum. Finds from the excavations in the former courtroom.

Chalice Well
Associations with healing and the Holy Grail.

The Abbot's Fish House
Fourteenth-century building.

The George and Pilgrims Hotel
Dating from the fourteenth century, a splendid example of a panelled facade. Many other historic buildings in the town.

Somerset Levels Museum
South of Wedmore at the Willow Garden Centre. Small exhibition of photographs and artifacts from recent excavations.

Shoe Museum, Street
Clark's factory.

is Burrow Mount or Burrow Mump, which is reputedly the site of King Alfred's island refuge from the Danes when his fortunes were at a low ebb. The $9\frac{1}{2}$-acre National Trust site has an unfinished eighteenth-century chapel on the summit. This chapel is on the site of an earlier one and it was once the site of a Norman fort.

Due north from here by way of quiet

Glastonbury Tor

Barrington Court

Packhorse bridge at Allerford, Minehead

minor roads is Westonzoyland. Here is another pumping station with an 1861 Easton and Amos steam pump and other items of interest from the days of steam-powered drainage. There is also a working blacksmith's forge.

Westonzoyland is famous, or infamous, as the place where the captured rebels were brought after the Battle of Sedgemoor in 1685. The parish register gives the beginning of the sad tale of vengeance. About five hundred prisoners from the battle were taken into the church. Twenty-two were hanged at once, four of them in chains. Colonel Kirke, one of the royalist officers, set out on a ruthless rounding up of suspected rebel sympathisers. One family had an elderly lady hauled away merely for rendering help to an injured man. In another family when the suspect was not found his brother was taken in his place. Colonel Kirke is reputed to have stated that it was the family that owed a life. Eventually over a thousand prisoners were held in various jails throughout the West Country. Five hundred people were condemned in both Taunton and Wells — the five hundred in Wells in only a single day! Many were hanged, drawn and quartered, then the remains were boiled in salt and preserved with pitch. The executions were public and the preserved remains were put on public display, often outside the victim's own house. To take the body down was an offence punishable by a period in the pillory. Many were transported to the West Indies to serve as slaves in the canefields including many who had been condemned to death. Some died on the trip out, some died due to the hard labour of the fields.

In 1688 another rebellion took place, this time successful. William III landed with a large army, and James II fled without a fight. The convicted rebels were reprieved and many returned to their homes.

The main road allows a speedy passage up to Street and Glastonbury. At one time Glastonbury may have been an island, or at least a peninsula and access was difficult, particularly in winter. Small boats sailed up the river; Joseph of Arimathea is said to have 'landed' and implanted his staff, which grew into the celebrated Christmas flowering Glastonbury Thorn.

Evidence of early occupation is ample and mysterious. Prehistoric occupation took place both on the Tor and on and around the lakes. Joseph and his eleven disciples landed one Christmas morning about AD 30. The first church, of wattle and daub, was built by them on the site of the present abbey ruins. The Romans grew vines on the southern slopes. King Ine built the first monastery in 688 and from then on the legends give way to recorded history. Legend links St Patrick with Glastonbury. King Arthur, and later Queen Guinevere, were reputedly buried here. The Chalice Well is linked with the Arthurian legends and the quest for the Holy Grail. It also has an ancient tradition of healing and in the eighteenth century this gave the town some reputation as a spa.

St Dunstan, who later became Archbishop of Canterbury, introduced Benedectine rule and from his appointment seems to stem the rise of the wealth and influence of the abbey.

One of the mysteries of the area and difficult to see except from the air, is the Glastonbury Zodiac. A circle fifteen miles across and centred on Butleigh, it has the signs of the zodiac as raised ridges on the ground. Why, how, or by whom it was created no

Glastonbury Tor

one seems to know.

Glastonbury Tor is a conical hill with a tower, the remains of a church, on the top. The Tor and St Michael's Tower dominate the surrounding countryside, and a climb to the top is rewarded by superb views.

Glastonbury has much to see. There are old houses worth looking at, and the churches are full of interest. The abbey ruins are, of course, prime tourist attractions, but the dedicated will also want to see the Abbey Barn, built in the fourteenth century, which is now the home of the Somerset Rural Life Museum. The exhibits include hand tools and horse age machinery, rural crafts, wheelwright's shop, cider making and peat digging. The Tribunal, a medieval courthouse dating back to 1400, where the abbots had considerable influence, is also a museum.

Chalice Well, or blood spring, lies at the foot of the Tor. Early Christian and Arthurian legend links it with healing and the quest for the Holy Grail. It is open all year, but afternoons only in winter.

The façade of the George and Pilgrims Hotel is regarded as one of the finest panelled designs and the hotel is a good example of an original inn. Founded in between 1327 and 1377 it was rebuilt about 1460 and has offered accommodation to pilgrims ever since.

Irregular mounds seen from the Godney road just outside town, are the site of a prehistoric lake village discovered in 1892. Probably dating from 150 BC the village was built on platforms above the swamps. Artifacts from the excavations are on show in the Tribunal Museum.

The surrounding peat moors have been commercially excavated for many years. Plans are afoot to create extensive recreational lakes and nature reserves when the peat is worked out. This will restore the area to the state which must have existed in the distant past before the monks took a hand in 'improving' the land to enhance the finances of the abbey.

The Somerset Levels Project has been excavating in the area for some years. There are extensive displays in the County Museum at Taunton but there was no local exhibition. The Project collaborated with a local peat company to set up a small museum at the Willow Garden Centre just south of Wedmore on the minor road to Shapwick. Peat cutting tools and some early photographs along with artifacts, diagrams and photographs of the excavations make up the displays. The main feature of the excavations are the ancient trackways that have existed from prehistoric times. The most recent excavation is of the Sweet Track, dated to 3,200 BC and thought to be the oldest road in the world.

Just to the south of Glastonbury lies Street, rather overshadowed by being so close by. It is nevertheless quite ancient, getting its name from the nearby Roman road or street. Two local families, the Clarks and the Moorlands, were mainly responsible for the present prosperity of the town. The Moorlands dealt in sheep skins, which they still do, and scoured the countryside for supplies. Clark's shoe factory has a very interesting museum. There may be seen displays of shoes dating from Roman times to the present day, and not just shoes but fashion plates, shoe buckles and shoe making machinery of the nineteenth century. Early advertising posters and a shoe snuff box collection make up a remarkable and unusual museum very well worth the visit.

3 Taunton and the Quantocks

On the A30 near the borders with Devon and Dorset is the small town of Chard. The town has Saxon origins and has been a borough since the thirteenth century. Almost the oldest building is the parish church, for in 1577 almost all of the town was burnt to the ground. Fore Street gives Chard a special character with a few of the buildings dating from the years just after the fire. The town hall, which is a focal point, is a Georgian building with a cupola, similar to the one at Bridport.

Old Town has narrow streets and abrupt corners to explore. The gram-

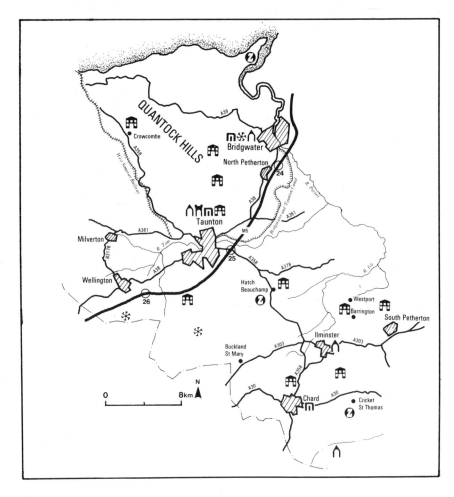

mar school was founded in 1671, though the building is older. Charles I passed by during the Civil War and bivouacked twice but there was no fighting. Judge Jeffreys hanged twelve Chard men following the Monmouth Rebellion. In the High Street is a plaque commemorating the inventor John Stringfellow. He made an aeroplane in 1847 and exhibited it at Crystal Palace in 1868. His models can be seen in the Science Museum in London. The trouble was that petrol, or aviation spirit, had not been refined. His engine relied on methylated spirit. John Stringfellow died without recognition.

At the heyday of the canals it was possible to take barges from Chard to Bridgwater. There is a museum in the town with exhibits showing local and industrial history.

Just to the north of the town, off the A358, is Hornsbury Mill. This nineteenth-century mill has been restored to working order, and there is a unique collection of bric-a-brac housed on the four floors of the mill building. The small grounds are attractive and there are ducks to feed on the mill pond. Chard offers trout fishing on the River Axe, as well as coarse fishing.

East towards Crewkerne the A30 climbs upward towards Windwhistle Hill. Here is a nine-hole golf course, and on the opposite side of the road is the village of Cricket St Thomas. The manor house was once the home of the Hood family; Admiral Hood was the most celebrated member of the family, his fame arising from his naval victories against the French in the eighteenth century.

Cricket St Thomas Wild Life Park was opened in 1967. It is now one of the leading wild life parks in the country. There is an aviary, and sixteen acres of gardens in addition to the large lawns. The Butterfly Breeding Unit allows the worldwide collection of

Hornsbury Mill, near Chard

Things to do around Chard

Cricket St Thomas Wildlife Park
One thousand acres of woodland and lakes. Domestic animals on the farm and wild animals in the park. Heavy horse centre and country life museum.

Chard
Museum in a restored Elizabethan cottage.

Hornsbury Mill
A nineteenth-century mill restored to working order. Small museum of bric-a-brac, attractive grounds and refreshments available in the restaurant.

Fishing
On the River Axe.

Dawlish Wake
Cider mill in a sixteenth-century barn, museum of farm implements and wagons.

Forde Abbey
Fifteenth-century Cistercian Monastery. Gardens, lakes and parkland. House and gardens open. Forde Abbey Fruit Gardens, pick your own fruit in season.

butterflies to live in natural surroundings, and the Country Life Museum has a collection giving an insight into obsolete crafts. A working dairy farm is on display and milking can be seen. The heavy horse centre is a thrilling sight as these magnificent animals help with the daily farm work or run free in the fields. There is a restaurant on the premises and visitors can also enjoy a traditional picnic on the site set aside for this purpose. As with many old manor houses the church is close by; there are many interesting features in this, one of the smallest churches in the country. Woodland and lakeside walks are provided, where the visitor can stroll and enjoy the exotic birds.

Three miles north of Cricket St Thomas is the village of Dawlish Wake. Here the cider mills of Perry Brothers can be visited in a unique sixteenth-century barn. There is a museum of farm bygones and a gift shop.

Four miles south-east of Chard is Forde Abbey, set in the lovely valley of the River Axe. The building was started early in the twelfth century but was not finally completed until the fifteenth century. It was a flourishing Cistercian monastery and the history of its rise to riches and noble learning makes fascinating reading. Abbot Chard added to the building between 1500 and 1536. At the dissolution of the monasteries, Abbot Chard gave the property to the king to save it from destruction. Much of the early building can still be seen including the refectory, the dormitory and the chapter house, which is now a chapel.

The house, last altered in 1650, contains a rich collection of furniture, pictures and tapestries. There are thirty acres of gardens, lakes and parkland, much of it the result of centuries of landscaping and planting. Forde Abbey Fruit Gardens offer the opportunity to pick strawberries, raspberries and currants in season, with the spectacular countryside as a backdrop.

Ilminster is about six miles northward from Chard. Ilminster means minster on the River Isle. The fifteenth-century parish church of St Mary is of splendid proportions; the tower is thought to have been modelled on Wells Cathedral. A plaque on the George Hotel commemorates the visit of Queen Victoria, even though she

Ilminster Church

Things to do round Ilminster

Ilminster
Fifteenth-century parish church.
Riverside walk.

Westport
Small village specially built as a
canal terminal.

East Lambrook Manor
Fifteenth-century manor with
gardens, nursery and fish garden.

Barrington Court
House and gardens open (limited).
The house was built in 1520, but
interior extensively restored this
century. Gardens laid out by
Gertrude Jekyll in the 1920s.

Castle Neroche
Country Park, Nature Trail and
picnic site.

was only a baby at the time. The old
grammar school was founded in 1586.
There was once a flourishing lace
making industry in the town, and flax
as well. The Saturday market has been
flourishing for many years. Judge
Jeffreys took a terrible retribution on
the local Speke family, whose elder son
led a troop in Monmouth's army. The
elder son escaped abroad, but Judge
Jeffreys hung the younger son instead
from a tree in the market place. A
walk from Ilminster starts near the
Minster Church, where a lane runs
south soon swinging west. Go to the
end then over the fields to Coldharbour, cross the river and turn right,
downstream. Cross the river back and
back again before crossing the main
road to continue downstream. At the
next footbridge cross the river again
and go south-east back to the town.

Westport, a few miles north, was
created as an inland port by the Parret
Navigation Company at the height of
the canal era. Goods of many kinds;
cider, wool, stone and willows went
out, with coal and machinery coming
in.

One mile south of Westport is
Barrington village and Barrington
Court (National Trust). The house was
built by Lord Daubeny in 1520 in the
local Ham stone, and little external
alteration has been made since. It has
twisted finials and late Gothic win-
dows. The seventeenth-century coach
house and stables have been converted
to a private dwelling. The house and
gardens have limited opening, with
no picnic facilities.

A pleasant drive through the lanes
eastward for three miles to East Lambrook with its manor, nursery and fish
garden. The manor is a fifteenth-
century house, again built of local

Ham stone. It is furnished with period furniture throughout. The house is only open in summer on Thursdays, but the gardens are open daily all year; they and the nursery are laid out as an Elizabethan cottage garden on a large scale.

Almost six miles due west of Ilminster is Castle Neroche and Neroche Forest. This was once one of the great Somerset 'forests', ie a hunting ground, not just an area covered with trees. Neroche Forest once covered five thousand acres. The castle was a prehistoric site. It was used by the Saxons just before the Norman invasion; then it was taken over by County Robert of Mortain, a half brother to William the Conqueror.

Wellington Monument

He built a timber tower and surrounded it by a timber palisade and deep ditches. Only twenty years later the site was abandoned in favour of Montacute, some twenty miles to the east. The forest is still over two thousand acres and is under the care of the Forestry Commission, who have laid out an attractive nature trail, and there is a picnic site in the forest park. The walk is 2½ miles long through mixed woodland with many streams, there is a short-cut back to the start for a walk of 1½ miles.

Castle Neroche is the eastern outpost of the Blackdown Hills. Priors Park picnic place is just to the west of the B3170 near Widcome. The setting is a former parkland set high on the hills, yet reasonably level and with an open grassy play area surrounded by oak, beech and larch.

East of Widcombe a road runs along the top of the hills, which in places marks the county boundary between Somerset and Devon to the south. To the north is The Vale of Taunton Deane. Near the western end of the hill is the Wellington Monument, an imposing obelisk built in 1818 to commemorate the exploits of the Duke of Wellington. The National Trust owns the long strip of land from the road to the obelisk, an area of just over twelve acres.

Past the monument and the crossroads, where the road turns sharply to the north a small lane leads ahead. This bridleway, later unfenced, makes a fine walk over Blackdown Common with splendid views all round. It is just over the border in Devon.

Any of the minor roads at the western end of Blackdown Hill go north, down off the hills, crossing the M5 motorway, and into Wellington, which is under three miles from the monument. Wellington lies on the A38, once described as 'the longest lane in Britain'. The town was saved from being throttled to death with traffic by the building of the M5 motorway. Between two and three hundred years ago weaving was being organised into an integrated industry from the scattered cottage industry that it was at that time. As in other parts of the west country, serge was the main product. Much of the cloth produced went to the Continent. A Wellington family of Quakers were the instigators of the integration of the weaving trade, and ran the ensuing firm for one hundred years. Then the business passed to the Fox family. As much of the business of the firm was on the Continent, members of both families spent a lot of time abroad learning the languages, and the firm's records contain many letters referring to the fact that business was conducted, if need be, in French, Dutch or German.

Light engineering and shopping came to the aid of the town as the weaving trade declined. Wellington has wide streets on each side of its central crossroads with a few Georgian houses. The classical town hall dominates the centre while the old church is at the eastern end. In the Perpendicular-style church is a stately tomb with a Corinthian pillared canopy. Here is buried Sir John Popham, the Lord Chief Justice when he died in 1607; he was the presiding judge at the trial of Guy Fawkes.

Wellington has a sports centre which has a 25-metre heated indoor pool, a multiple sports hall, squash, sauna, and a dry ski slope. The sports centre runs 'Learn To' courses, and has the usual refreshment facilities. There is a wide variety of shops in the town with free parking near the town centre.

Things to do in Taunton

Taunton Castle
The scene of Judge Jeffreys's Bloody Assize.

Castle Museum
The County Museum and also the Somerset Light Infantry Museum.

Tudor House
Fore Street, now a licensed restaurant.

Shire Hall
Built in the nineteenth century in Elizabethan style. Also three ancient churches and seventeenth-century almshouses.

Telecommunications Museum
The exhibits illustrate the history of the evolution of communications.

Cinemas
Two, one with two screens.

Brewhouse Theatre.

Sports
Two eighteen-hole golf courses, tennis, indoor swimming pool, bowls, riding at Obridge Stables, horse racing and polo at Orchard Portman, one mile south of the town outskirts, fishing at Clatworth reservoir near the Brendon Hills (Chapter 4) and at Hawkridge reservoir in the Quantocks.

Some six miles north-east along the A38 is the Somerset county town of Taunton, also accessible from junction 25 off the M5 motorway, and giving its name to the lovely Vale of Taunton Deane.

Taunton has always been at the centre of history in the area, no doubt because of the position the town occupies in the centre of the valley,

Castle Bow, Taunton

with a river to make it more accessible. King Ine of Wessex fortified Taunton in AD 710. Twelve years later according to the *Anglo Saxon Chronicle* 'Queen Ethelburga razed Taunton'.

During medieval times Taunton flourished under the tolerant rule of the Bishops of Winchester. The fact that Taunton belonged to Winchester led to the town having a somewhat odd position through the years. The large ecclesiastical houses of Glastonbury and Wells owned much of Somerset and that led to smaller places than Taunton being developed as county towns. Ilchester, though much smaller, was county town for a while, as was Somerton.

Taunton Castle was built during the twelfth century when Henry of Blois was both Abbot of Glastonbury and Bishop of Winchester. He built a massive Norman keep which has now

disappeared. Parts of the castle, especially the later additions, now house the county museum. The Great Hall of the castle was the scene of Judge Jeffreys's Bloody Assize, when as presiding judge he sent 150 people to their deaths, and many more to transportation. His ghost is said to walk on September nights (September was the month of the trials).

After these stirring times Taunton picked up the threads of its interrupted trade as a clothing centre. Serge making was predominant, later silk took over and the town became famous for its shirts and collars.

Since Stuart times rebuilding has occurred with most of the town architecture being Georgian or Victorian. The town centre now contains many modern buildings. Taunton is still a busy market town with an excellent shopping centre.

A pleasant walk, from near the railway station, is along the canal and back along the river bank. It is possible to make this walk three miles long by using the A38 for a quarter of a mile south from the canal to the river. By walking to Creech St Michael the distance would be six miles. The really energetic could continue to Charlton, across the fields south to the river, and then back to the town, for a walk of ten miles.

Trull is 1½ miles south of Taunton on a minor road. The church, which dates from the thirteenth century, has some of the best examples of wood carving in the area and is worth a visit.

Also in Taunton and not to be missed are the Tudor House in Fore Street and the seventeenth-century almshouses. Among the modern attractions are two eighteen-hole golf courses, bowls and tennis, fishing and an indoor swimming pool. There is a

Things to do around Taunton

Wellington
Sports centre and dry ski slope, heated indoor swimming pool.

The Wellington Monument
Downland walk on the Blackdown Hills.

Staple Hill
Permanent orienteering course.

Priors Park Picnic Site
Seven miles south of Taunton just off the B3170.

Walks in Taunton Deane
Booklet from the information office.

West Somerset Railway
(See also Chapter 4) Trips from Bishops Lydeard to Minehead.

Poundisford Park
Tudor House, gardens deer park and lunch or cream teas in the Tudor kitchen.

Hestercombe Gardens
Orangery, Rose Garden and Dutch Garden.

Hatch Court
A mansion in the Palladian style in Bath stone, fine stone staircase. The house also has a small Canadian military museum and a deer park.

West Hatch Bird Sanctuary
Bird and animal sanctuary run by the RSPCA.

Cider Works
Sheppy and Son near Bradford on Tone.

Memorial Statue, Vivary Park, Taunton

cinema and theatre, the Brewhouse Theatre and Art Centre. The castle grounds are also the venue for Shakespearian productions. In the county museum, in the castle, are natural history and archaeological exhibits and a fine Roman mosaic. A visual history of the county is given in the Somerset Light Infantry Museum. There are paintings and a collection of extinct mammals from the Mendip caves. The museum is open daily in summer, but closed on Mondays in winter.

An unusual attraction is the Telecommunications Museum, where the exhibits include a selection of telegraph and telephone equipment, illustrating the history of telecommunications. From behind the castle an attractive walk follows the banks of the River Tone, while in Vivary Park beyond the High Street there are pleasant gardens with a jogging trail, a model railway and a model boating pond.

The area round Taunton is the fruit

Mr Bob Hughes, Assistant Warden, with two orphan badgers, West Hatch Animal Sanctuary

country with its fertile land that made Taunton and Norton Fitzwarren famous names in the world of cider. Cider is still made at Norton Fitzwarren by the Taunton Cider Company. Farmhouse cider has been made since makers came with the invading Norman armies. The craft of cider making became concentrated in larger establishments as the drink's popularity grew and the smaller farmhouse producers have mostly gone out of business. Just over four miles west from Taunton on the A38 is the establishment of R. J. Sheppy and Son, makers of farmhouse cider. Visitors can see the vat store and press room of a small traditional cider works. Over forty acres of orchards may be viewed along with a small farm and the cider museum.

Two miles south of the town, and signposted off the B3170 road, is Poundisford Park, a small early Tudor mansion with fine plaster ceilings which are complemented by period furniture and paintings. There are also interesting small collections of costumes and porcelain. The gardens are plainly laid out in the Tudor fashion and have views of the Blackdown and Quantock Hills. As this was the former deer park of Taunton Castle there are woodland walks to enjoy. Lunches and cream teas are available in the Tudor Kitchen.

About four miles south of Taunton on the A358 road towards Ilminster is the village of Hatch Beauchamp. To the west down narrow lanes is the RSPCA animal centre and wildlife field unit (signposted off the main road). It is impossible to say what might be found here as anything and everything is cared for by the resident staff. Stray dogs and cats, of course, are accepted by the centre from the local police forces. However it is quite possible to find anything in temporary residence from a dormouse to a deer. The aim of the centre is eventually to return wild creatures to the wild after they have been restored to health. A small exhibition of pictures dealing with the work of the National Oiled Seabird Cleaning Centre, which is also housed here, is worth a visit. The centre is pleased to receive visitors who are in sympathy with their aims and realise that most of the animals are not domesticated.

Across the main road is Hatch Court, a fine mansion in the Palladian style and built of Bath stone, with its nearby medieval church of St John the Baptist. In the house there is a magnificent stone staircase. Seventeenth and eighteenth century furniture, paintings, a china room and a small Canadian Military museum make up the attractions.

Things to do around the Quantock Hills

Walks
Nine-mile ridge walk from West Quantoxhead. Walks from the A39 car parking areas at the north of the hills. Forest trail and picnic site signposted from Nether Stowey. Coast Walk from Stogursey past Hinkley Point to Lilstock.

Coleridge Cottage, Nether Stowey
The poet's parlour is open in the afternoons.

Kilve Church

Crowcombe
Village and church.

Halsway Manor
Folk music and dance centre.

North of Taunton rises the massif of the Quantock Hills, with the highest point at 358 in (1,200 ft). On the eastern side the slopes are gentle as the central plateau gives way to rolling hills. To the west the slopes are much steeper and the whole area is famous for the wooded combes which cut into the hills on all sides. A well-known walk along the Quantock crest is one of the joys of the area and is a favourite walk for ramblers. It is almost nine miles long and gives fantastic views on all sides. The main A39 Bridgwater to Minehead road squeezes round between the northern end of the hills and the sea. Along here are car parking spaces and tracks leading up to Pardlestone Hill, Longstone Hill and Beacon Hill. It is quite a steep climb so take it gently with plenty of time to look at the views.

The picnic site provided by the Forestry Commission as part of their forest park recreation scheme can be approached from the A39 at Nether Stowey, from where it is signposted. Situated in Rams Combe it is a very pleasant streamside site in a valley bottom surrounded by conifers and mature Douglas fir. Starting at the picnic site is the Quantock Forest Trail, a three-mile walk giving forest views and climbing through mixed woodland with the remnants of an old oak coppice. It crosses a stream and climbs to a fine viewpoint. There is varied bird life in the forest and a chance of spotting red deer.

Also at Nether Stowey is Coleridge Cottage, owned by the National Trust. Samuel Taylor Coleridge lived in the cottage from 1796 to 1799, and it was here he wrote *The Ancient Mariner*. Only the parlour is open in the afternoons from April to September, except Friday and Saturday. There are no

Coleridge Cottage,
Nether Stowey

facilities at the cottage, but meals and teas are available in the village.

Two miles away towards the coast is the village of Stogursey. Although it is a quiet place now, in the twelfth century the local lord, called Fulke de Breaute, gathered in his castle a band of robbers who terrorized the surrounding countryside before he was brought to justice. The remains of the castle can still be seen. From Stogursey there is a walk over the fields, or down the lanes if the going is muddy, to Wick and then to Stolford on the coast. A left turn along the footpath gives a good close view of Hinkley Point nuclear power station. On this featureless stretch of coast the mighty

strength of the square buildings match the long horizontal lines of the coast. These coastal paths were made many years ago when the coastguards made regular patrols. From here the coast path goes right along to East Quantoxhead about seven miles away, or it is possible to cut back from the power station or the villages of Burton or Lilstock. One can turn back up to the village of Kilve and have a look at the church and the remains of the chantry. If you approach by car from the main road there is a good beach down the track beyond the church.

On the other side of the hills quietly tucked away on a minor road is the village of Crowcombe. Comfortably

| Things to do around Bridgwater |

St Mary's Church
A fourteenth-century church with
Jacobean screen and a painting of
the Descent from the Cross.

Castle Street
Georgian Houses.

The Old Docks
Docks and warehouses of this
historic port.

Admiral Blake Museum
Exhibits relating to the admiral's
career, the history of the town and
the Battle of Sedgemoor.

**The Friary, Town Hall, Hospital of
St John**
All are interesting buildings.

Modern facilities
Fishing for trout on Durleigh reservoir, open-air swimming pool, a
cinema, tennis and bowls.

Bird Sanctuary, Stert
Also nature reserve.

Golf
Nine-hole course near Enmore, just
outside town.

Barford Park
Queen Anne stone and red brick
building in a large pleasant garden.

Fyne Court
Gardens, nature trail and woodland
walks, also visitor centre for the
Quantock Hills.

nestling against the south-western face
of the hills, it is considered by many to
be the gem of all the Quantock villages. Crowcombe is dominated by the
eighteenth-century brick and Ham
stone mansion of Crowcombe Court.

The church, like so many in the
county, has some magnificent bench
ends which enhance the interest and
are splendid, even by the high standards of Somerset. The carvings include a mermaid and two men spearing
a dragon. The church is mostly Per-
pendicular of a high standard. There is
a fine south aisle and a fan-vaulted
southern porch.

Not far away north-eastward is the
hamlet of Halsway and Halsway
Manor, a historic house with some fine
decorated ceilings and panelling. It is
open throughout the year, unless it is
being used for a conference, so check
locally first before visiting. The prime
use of the house now is as a folk music
and dance centre.

North-east of the Quantock Hills is
Bridgwater, which derives its name
from the Norman knight Burgh
Walter, who was given the estate following the Conquest. The castle was
built to guard what was probably the
best crossing of the Parrett estuary if
the traveller wished to avoid the worst
of the mud. As the Danes were re-
treating from a defeat by the Saxons
under King Alfred it was probably to
Bridgwater that they came. This was in
the ninth century and the place was
fortified at that time. In the Civil War
Lord Goring surrendered at Bridgwater
in 1645 to Cromwell after a defeat at
Langport by Cromwell's New Army.
The Norman castle was demolished
after the restoration. St Mary's
Church, dating from the fourteenth
century, is the town's sole remaining
medieval building. It was from this
church tower that James, Duke of
Monmouth, saw the Royalist army
approaching and planned the unsuccessful surprise attack which led to the
Battle of Sedgemoor in 1685. The
church has a graceful tall spire and

*Georgian Houses, Castle Street,
Bridgewater*

among its many features are a
Jacobean screen in a side chapel and a
painting of the Descent from the
Cross, attributed to an unknown
Italian artist.

A Georgian area survives from the
days when it was planned for Bridgwater to rival Bristol as a port. The
best group is in Castle Street between
King Street and the Quay. Taunton
was linked by canal and Bridgwater
was the main port of entry for much of
central and west Somerset, with barge
traffic going many miles up the rivers
feeding into the Parrett. The old docks
with their warehouses can be seen in
this historic port, which saw the Bristol
Channel paddle steamers plying regularly to South Wales and Burnham on
Sea.

Outside the market hall is a statue to
Admiral Blake, a son of the town born
in 1599. He won fame as a soldier
defending Taunton during a one-year
siege. Later he became Admiral of The
Fleet to Cromwell, a position he held
for nine years. Some historians rate
him second only to Lord Nelson. The
Blake museum has much material relating to his career, with other displays
on the history of the town and district
with archaeology and the Battle of
Sedgemoor being featured. The Friary,
the Town Hall and Hospital of St John
are also worth noting.

Modern Bridgwater has a cinema
and an open-air swimming pool; fishing is available close by along with
tennis and bowls.

Downstream, is the village of Combwich, possibly an unloading place for
the larger ships not wishing to risk
coming further upstream. This was the
last ford across the river and large
numbers of skeletons have been un-
earthed at various times below the old

ford indicating a large battle. A favourite topic of controversy for antiquarians is whether this was Kynuit, the site of a Saxon victory over the Danes. Beyond Combwich is Stert, a hamlet almost in the Bristol Channel. Stert has a bird sanctuary and nature reserve. The tides race in at a phenominal rate over the mud flats which extend over two miles offshore, so make sure you keep your feet dry. A footpath goes from Castle Field in Bridgwater along the riverbank down to Stert, making a twelve-mile walk. Short cuts back can be made through the village of Chilton Trinity.

Just outside Bridgwater, on a minor road south of the A39, is the village of Durleigh and the nearby reservoir offers trout fishing. A little over a mile beyond and just before the village of Enmore, is a nine-hole golf course. Beyond the village the next turning right, north, towards Four Forks leads to Barford Park. Barford House is a small Queen Anne mansion in stone and red brick set in a large garden. The rooms with contemporary furniture are in daily family use. There is a walled flower garden, woodland and water gardens, and an archery glade.

Two and a half miles south is the hamlet of Broomfield, and Fyne Court Gardens (National Trust). These are the pleasure grounds that were attached to the house, which was demolished following a disastrous fire in 1898. The remnants of the building, the library and the music room are still in use, the latter being used for lectures and social events. The Somerset Trust for Nature Conservation has its headquarters here and the grounds are a nature reserve. There are pleasant woodland walks and a nature trail booklet is available. A lake, walled garden, two ponds and a small arboretum are among the attractions.

4 Exmoor and the Somerset Coast

North West Somerset includes Exmoor. Some of the 265 square miles of the moor is in Devon but just over 70 per cent is in Somerset. The highest point is Dunkery Beacon at 443m (1,705 ft). This is splendid walking country and there are many fine walks in the area, high ridges on the moors or sheltered valleys following the fast flowing streams.

On the coastal strip there is the Somerset and North Devon Coast Path, now extended into the South West Peninsula Path which runs all the way round the coast to Bournemouth. The section in Somerset runs from the county line to Minehead and offers fine

sea views. To the north and east can be seen Wales, the islands of Steep and Flat Holme, Brean Down, the Mendips and the Brendon and Quantock hills. There are many short walks and nature trails in the area, a visit to one of the five information offices (some run by the National Trust and some by the National Park) will provide leaflets to all the walks.

At County Gate on the A39, there is a car park and an information office open in the summer. Just over the border and on the seaward side of the road is Old Barrow, or Burrow, one of the few Roman remains on Exmoor. Raiding across the channel from South

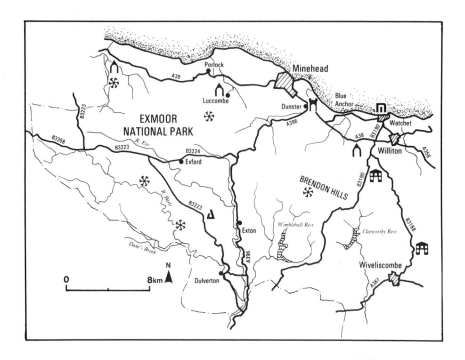

Oare Church, Exmoor. Site of Lorna Doone's wedding

Wales was a threat the Romans seem to have taken seriously. This small fort was garrisoned by about eighty legionaries under command of a centurion. From the car park at County Gate a hut circle and a viewpoint are not far away towards Lynton.

Badgeworthy Water forms the boundary between Somerset and Devon. This is Lorna Doone country, made famous by R. D. Blackmore's novel. East from County Gate the first turning right, leads down to Oare church, which was the scene of Lorna Doone's interrupted wedding. Inside the church is a memorial to the author. At the tiny hamlet of Malmesmead, turn right at the church where there is a picnic site and a gift shop. A pony trekking

stable completes this tiny hamlet. By going upstream the Doone Valley can be reached, the lower part of Hoccombe Combe, just before Badgeworth Hill. One may walk up the road to reach a public footpath, to the Doone Valley, which rejoins the river higher up. Or pay the local farmer a modest fee to follow the river all the way, for a 4-mile round trip.

Did the Doones exist, were they fact or legend? Well, the Doones did exist and Jon Ridd went to school at Tiverton, but Blackmore's masterpiece is a work of fiction. However there *was* much lawlessness and feuding in many country areas and the wilds of Exmoor remained that way longer than most due to the difficulty of access to that area. Possibly adding fuel to the flames was the action of one landowner in bringing in Scottish families, dispossessed during the Highland clearances. These migrants, one can imagine, may not have got on very well with the locals. The landowner hoped the hardy northerners would more easily come to terms with the wild country and help tame it.

The rivers that run north from Exmoor, the East Lyn, Farley Water, Hoaroak Water and Badgeworth Water are fed by many tributaries. To the north the moor is steep and in times of heavy rain these rivers can rise very swiftly. Northward from The Chains, which lie west from Brendon Two Gates, are many small streams fed by the marshy area below the ridge. From the official annual rainfall figures: Minehead 35in, Dulverton 60in and The Chains 80in, it is obvious that the area up on the moors can be quite damp. In normal times the peat soaks up the rain to release it gradually, draining into the streams. However if rain is heavy and continuous then

Things to see on Exmoor

Oare Church
Oare, near Lynton. Set in a lovely wooded valley and made famous by R. D. Blackmore's novel.

Lorna Doone
The church was the setting for Lorna Doone's wedding, a memorial to the author is in the church.

The Doone Valley
The home of the famous band of outlaws described by R. D. Blackmore. A picnic site lies at the foot of the main valley, a quality gift shop close by the car park, and an establishment selling prepacked picnics. A public footpath can be used by climbing up one side of the valley. To follow the private riverside path a modest fee is payable to the farmer.

Landacre Bridge
A fine stone bridge in a moorland setting. Spanning the River Barle south of B3223 with car parking space and riverside walks.

Exford
Staghounds meet in season, enquire locally.

Tarr Steps
Crossing the River Barle, between Hawkridge and Liscombe. A fine example of a clapper bridge.

The Caractacus Stone
A Roman relic near Spire Cross on the B3223. Possibly a memorial to the Celtic chief Caractacus. Though defeated and captured by the Romans they were so impressed by his noble bearing that his life was spared.

Dulverton
A market town and home of the Exmoor National Park Centre at Exmoor House, which houses an information centre and craft studio for silks and woollens.

Luccombe
A thatched church and Cloutsham Nature Trail, a three-mile walk over moor and through oak woods.

Dunkery Beacon
Exmoor's highest point, just under a mile from Dunkery Hill car park.

flooding in the lower reaches occurs as the peat on the moors can absorb no more water, and the rain runs straight off. The water from the majority of the northern watershed runs down through Lynton and Lynmouth. Such conditions caused the disaster of 1952 when floods almost destroyed Lynmouth.

All this is the harsh wintry side of the moor far removed from the mood which caused R. D. Blackmore to write 'the land lies softly'. From the car park area on the B3223 near Brendon Common a signposted footpath leads to the Doone Valley and over the moor, for a walk of about four miles there and back.

The smooth hills of central Exmoor near Simonsbath are coated with blue moor grass or tawny deer sedge. The valleys may be bare and smooth, marshy or tree covered. Often the headwaters of the rivers run from peaty channels, many stained with iron ore. The mood of the streams is different in the valleys where the peat channels become trout streams.

In spring the wooded valleys wear carpets of bluebells surrounded by banks where the earlier primroses grow. At all times of the year grey-green lichen can be found on the rocks and trees. The Exe and the Barle, on the southern side of the watershed, are gentler rivers as they wind through wooded valleys on their way to the south coast. Along the coast and the heather moors can be found miniature forests of cotton grass. Pink orchids and red lichens form brighter patches against the gentler colours of sphagnum moss and sundews found round the marshy areas.

To many visitors one of the greatest charms of Exmoor is its variety, which has an influence on the wildlife of the area. Exmoor ponies, whose colour ranges from red-brown to dark brown with black tail and mane, are often seen. They are not wild, in the sense that they do not belong to anyone, and their interests are looked after by the Exmoor Pony Society. Much more difficult to spot are the wild red deer. It is believed that between 800 and 1,000 belong to this, the largest herd of red deer in England, and their territory takes in the Quantock Hills. One of the earliest packs of staghounds is believed to have been kept by Hugh Pollard in 1598, and there is little doubt that regular hunting has taken place since the middle of the seventeenth century. The Devon and Somerset Staghounds meet regularly at Exford.

There are many foxes and rabbits, and badgers are common though they prefer the lower areas to the open moor. Grey squirrels appear all over the area and other residents include stoats, weasels, hedgehogs, hares and moles. As for bird life a better reserve could not have been built, the list seems impossibly long, as the great variety of landscape: open moor,

Tarr Steps, Exmoor

woodland, streams, and coast, provide such an abundance of habitat in a relatively small area. Dipper and Grey Wagtail can be seen along the fast flowing streams. Along the Barle Kingfishers and Moorhens nest. In many of the waters herons fish, and there is a heronry at Coppleham Cross near Winsford. There are Sandpipers and Sand Martins, Chats, Warblers and Finches. Open moorland makes up just over 25 per cent of the whole National Park. Relatively small numbers of both Red and Black Grouse survive on the moor. While Snipe, Curlew and Lapwing are regular nesters, the Meadow Pipit and Skylark are the most common. Whinchat and Wheatear, and the Ring Ousel are summer visitors, a few Merlin nest on the moor. Rarer species like the Hen Harrier, Rough Legged Buzzard, Great Grey Shrike and Snow Bunting have all been spotted occasionally. In addition all the small birds associated with the English countryside may be found, the Robin, Wren and Blackbird, Chaffinch, Greenfinch and all the Tit family to name but a few.

History can be seen on all sides round the moor and in the villages and towns. There are Bronze Age barrows such as Aldermans Barrow north of Exford or Chapmans Barrow, as well as earthworks such as Cow Castle and Mounsey both beside the River Barle. Cow Castle can be reached by a two-mile riverside bridleway south from Simonsbath. From Hawkridge church a road used as a public path follows Hawkridge ridge south-easterly to dive down to the river where there is a footbridge crossing to Mounsey Castle. North of the village of Hawkridge is Tarr Steps, do not be confused by the map, there is no road bridge and the car park is on the northern side. Tarr Steps is a fine example of a clapper bridge, large flat stones placed across the tops of upright stones. These clapper bridges date from the medieval times, so they have obviously stood the test of time. Approach from Winsford and cross the B3223 at Spire Cross, there is plenty of parking space and Tarr Steps Farm has morning coffee, lunch and cream teas.

Close by Spire Cross is the Caractacus Stone left mysteriously by the Romans. Caractacus was a Celtic chief who the Romans defeated and took prisoner. They were, however, so impressed by his noble bearing that they did not kill him, the usual fate of chiefs during Roman invasions. The inscription on the stone is translated as 'a descendant of Caractacus'. Caractacus was a common Celtic name, but the stone is a genuine relic of the fifth or sixth century AD. It lies just within the boundary of a piece of National Trust land that encompasses the top of Winsford Hill; one mile north-west along the main road is the summit (426m), a viewpoint and the Wambarrows.

More recent are the packhorse bridges at Dunster and Allerford, which is near Porlock. Most of the churches are medieval as are many of the farm buildings. Exmoor has no relics of the Neolithic period to rival Stonehenge. There are however many stone circles though they are not spectacular and have many stones missing. Solitary standing stones are numerous, though it is difficult to prove which are antiquities and which have been erected in more recent centuries as rubbing posts for cattle.

Exmoor was a royal forest and remained almost undisturbed until the 1800s. In the sixteenth century there were some 40,000 sheep on the moor, which is heavy usage even for today's standards. The Knight family were principally responsible for much of the moor as it appears today with its pattern of scattered farms and enclosures, which they created. In earlier times there were no roads on the moor and transport was by packhorse. John Knight had nearly thirty miles of new roads, and a similar length of boundary walls, constructed. He had his headquarters at Simonsbath which grew from an isolated farmhouse to a small village. The family introduced arable farming to the area round Simonsbath though grazing was predominant. John Knight's son, Sir Frederick, prospected for minerals. Little was found except for iron, and for a while there was an iron mine near the village and a railway was started, but never completed. The iron mines here were closed in 1860, they reopened briefly early this century but finally closed for good in 1914.

There were iron mines on the Brendon Hills; in the mid-eighteenth century there were about fourteen mines in production. The ore went by railway to Watchet and on to South Wales. Traces of the railway can still be found.

The villages of Exmoor hide in the valleys and sheltered combes, their white or grey stone houses often having the weather end to the west. In the villages are a variety of attractive churches and cosy inns. The churches have thier own individual attractions, from the tiny church at Oare to the larger parish church of Porlock, which has a truncated spire, and Dunster which is a double conventual church.

Before leaving this area, try to visit Landacre Bridge, a fine local stone bridge in a moorland setting. From the car park just south of the bridge a footpath goes downstream to Withy-

Landacre Bridge, Exmoor

pool, a round trip of about four miles. Up through Withypool village is a cosy little pub for refreshments before walking back again.

The road descends from the moor to Dulverton. By the river bridge is Exmoor House and the Exmoor National Park information centre where maps, photographs and other items of interest are displayed and experienced staff are on hand to answer enquiries. Guided walks, organised by the Park Authority and led by volunteer guides, are available on most days in the summer. Dulverton is a small country town bustling with farmers, tourists, huntsmen and fishermen. The town once had a Norman fort, Mounsey, or so it is said, but it seems remote from the present town. The remains of St Nicholas Priory are on top of the hill north-west of the town.

From Dulverton the A396 is a pleasant drive, northwards along the River Exe valley towards Wheddon Cross. This valley is the boundary between Exmoor and the Brendon Hills. For the last few miles the road follows the River Quarme, but north of Wheddon Cross the road starts to follow the River Avill towards Dunster. At Wheddon Cross turn onto the B3224, but soon turn off going up to Dunkery Gate and back to the moor. Just over three miles from the village is a car park and a viewpoint looking northwards to the coast. Leave the car and walk up the gentle rise to Exmoor's highest point, Dunkery Beacon. Dunkery is on National Trust land; in 1944 Sir Richard Acland, of a famous Exmoor family (an ancestor Sir Thomas Acland had been a Warden of The Forest) gave nearly 10,000 acres of his estate to the National Trust. This has been extended by other gifts and

Dunster Yarn Market, with Castle in the background

purchases into the Holnicote Estate of over 12,000 acres. The estate has nearly 7,000 acres of moorland and includes some of the loveliest parts of the area.

Just over 1½ miles due north, down a steep hill, is Cloutsham nature trail, a three-mile walk over moorland and through oak woods. Lower down is the hamlet of Luccombe with an unusual thatched church.

Dunster has a fine main street with the castle dominating one end, guarding the valley, and the seventeenth-century yarn market at the other end. During the Civil War the Royalists held the castle for 160 days against a siege by the Parliamentarians. This was the Royalists' last stronghold in Somerset as they retreated west. The castle, started by William de Mohun soon after the Norman invasion, was built on the site of a Saxon fort, and was remodelled in the nineteenth century. In 1376 the castle was bought by Lady Elizabeth Luttrell and it remained in the hands of the Luttrell family until in 1975 Lt Col G. W. F. Luttrell gave the property to the National Trust.

Among the many features of the castle are the carved elm staircase and the elaborate seventeenth-century plaster ceiling in the dining room. There is a fine collection of English furniture and a unique set of sixteenth-century leather hangings is on show in the banqueting hall. Outdoors are terraces of sub-tropical plants, with fine views of the Bristol Channel and the moors. Nearby is Dunster Castle mill, on the site of a mill mentioned in the Domesday Book. The present mill dates from the eighteenth century. It was restored in 1979 and can be reached from Mill Lane, the car park, or the castle gardens. The Yarn Market, built by George Luttrell about 1600, is a covered market used for

---

Places of interest on the Brendon Hills

Wimbleball Lake
Woodland walks, fly fishing, a picnic site and a nature reserve, also model sailing, canoeing and rowing.

Nettlecombe Court
A field study centre only open Thursdays and by appointment. It was the ancestral home of the Raleigh and Trevelyan families from the sixteenth century.

Lype Hill
Picnic site near Heath Poult Cross close to Lype Hill summit, at 423 m (1,390 ft) the highest point on the Brendons.

---

displaying the smooth 'kersey' cloth manufactured in the village. Look for a hole in a rafter made by a cannon shot during the Civil War siege.

The nearby Luttrell Arms is a medieval building and may have been the home, at one time, of the Abbot of Cleeve. The old dovecote, probably dating from the twelfth century, still has the revolving ladder used to reach the nesting boxes. There is a National Trust Information office and a shop at the castle, and it is possible to picnic in the park. The church, which was formerly part of the priory, has the longest rood screen in England. Conygar Tower, on the nearby hill, is not a medieval building but is Georgian Gothic.

The Brendon Hills are included in the Exmoor National Park. However little open moorland remains as this lower land has been fenced and improved for many generations. The result is high rolling fields and woodlands, the highest point being Lype Hill, at 423m (1,390 ft). There is a picnic site not far from the summit from where it is possible to take a walk through the woods. A climb up the combe, leads out onto Lype Common and up to the summit. A detour can be made on the way back to make an almost circular walk.

Lype Hill is the highest point in Somerset after Exmoor itself and there are fine views from the top over the

Right: The Gatehouse, Cleeve Abbey

Below: Cleeve Abbey

Things to see near the Brendon Hills

Gaulden Manor
A twelfth-century manor house once the home of the Turbevilles of Bere Regis. Open Easter and May to September, Thursday, Sunday and Bank Holidays. Off the B3188 near Tolland.

Combe Sydenham Hall
An Elizabethan house once the home of Elizabeth Sydenham, wife of Sir Francis Drake. Gardens, a deer park, corn mill and water wheel, woodland walks. Open May to October.

Combe Fisheries
At Combe Sydenham, a modern trout hatchery using ponds laid out when Sir Francis Drake married Elizabeth Sydenham.

Cleeve Abbey
A well preserved Cistercian abbey, small but with interesting features. Heraldic tiled pavement, timber roof and medieval wall paintings.

Old Cleeve
The sheepskin workshops of John Wood and Son. Guided tours of the workshops show the processing from raw skin to finished rugs and mats.

moors to the west. The nearby villages of Kingsbridge and Luxborough once provided accommodation for the miners on the Brendon Hills. Mining went on sporadically for many years; the mid-nineteenth century was the heyday when a mining village grew up on Brendon Hill. It was virtually owned by the mine owners and as it was a temperance village, thirsty miners had to walk to Raleigh Cross to get a drink. There was even a railway down to Watchet to ship the iron ore across to South Wales. This line closed finally just about the time of World War I. The village had a mission church, two Nonconformist chapels, a general shop and a warehouse. There was even a Temperance Hotel which no doubt was the headquarters of the Brendon Hill and Gupworthy Temperance Society and the Brendon Hill Teetotal Drum and Fife Band.

All the miners have gone now, but traces remain of the village and the railway, which had a very steep incline down its higher reach. Sea View House which once housed the mine 'captains' still stands, as does the Methodist Chapel to the west of Raleigh Cross Inn. However, Beulah Terrace, a row of miners' houses is in ruins. The great incline down to Comberow will probably never be obliterated from the landscape, such a large work will leave its traces probably for ever. A ruined winding house, once used to haul up the mine trucks, stands by the side of the incline.

The minor road via Roadwater continues on to Washford. Just before the main road is a car park serving Cleeve Abbey. This was a Cistercian abbey founded by the Earl of Lincoln towards the end of the twelfth century. Sufficient remains for the visitor to get a good impression of what a modestly sized abbey was like. Nowhere, not even at any of the other Cistercian houses, do the domestic buildings survive as well as at Cleeve. The combined gatehouse and almonry stands, the dormitory stairs and the monks' common room. A splendid wagon roof covers the hall, medieval wall paintings and a pavement with heraldic tiles are among the notable features. Possibly the main reason why the abbey is so well preserved is that it was held in high esteem by the local gentry. At the

Watchet, The Old Market House, now a museum

time of the dissolution they put in an unsuccessful plea for the continuance of the house. The seventeen monks were found to be above average in the work they did for charity and had a good reputation for being honest and hardworking.

On the opposite side of the hills is Wimbleball Lake, the largest lake in the area. It is over two miles long, winding round the hills. It has been created by the South West Water Authority as a reservoir by damming the River Hadden, and facilities for recreation are provided. Set among some of the most beautiful scenery of Exmoor there are glorious views, woodland walks and a nature reserve. A picnic site is provided with plenty of space for children to play, set against the colourful spectacle of the sailing boats. The lake is kept stocked with fish for fly fishermen to test their skills.

Approach from the A396 and Brompton Regis or the B3190 by way of Upton to Haddon Hill where there is a parking space for the viewpoint south towards Wellington and Tiverton. The National Park Authority has an information office at the lake.

On the B3188 Watchet to Taunton road there are three places of interest to visit. Working southwards they are Nettlecombe Court, Combe Sydenham Hall, Combe Fisheries and Gaulden Manor.

Combe Sydenham Hall, an Elizabethan manor, was built in 1580. It is a family home and is in the process of restoration. It was the home of Elizabeth Sydenham, the wife of Sir Francis Drake. On view in the Great Hall is Drake's cannonball. Legend says that Elizabeth tired of waiting for Sir Francis to return. She was going to marry another. A meteorite struck the

Things to see on the Somerset Coast

Watchet
Docks, museum, fifteenth-century church.

Dunster
Castle dating from the thirteenth century open April to September. Picnics in the park, deer park. The yarn market built in 1609 in the village street and Gallox Bridge, a pack horse bridge at the southern end of the village. The Old Dovecote dating from the twelfth century open daily Easter to mid-October. Town trail.

Selworthy
Picturesque village of thatched cottages, owned by the National Trust.

Minehead
Open-air swimming pool, theatre, bathing and boating, sea fishing can be arranged, tennis, bowls and an eighteen-hole golf course. Old-world harbour with quay and fishermens' chapel. Firm sandy beach. There is a lifeboat house to see at the harbour. 'Little England', a model of a typical English country town complete with miniature railway. Open daily from May to September.

West Somerset Railway
Steam trains on Britain's longest privately owned railway.

Craft Workshops
There are eleven in the area ranging from the potteries to silk and wool clothing.

Walks
From the sea front at Minehead coast paths go to Dunster, three miles, and Watchet, seven miles. Nature trails. Guided walks.

path in front of her as she was on the way to church. She took this as a sign to wait, and the meteorite is now known as Drake's cannonball. There is an Elizabethan garden to stroll around with a corn mill complete with water mill. Car parking is free, there are woodland walks to enjoy and a deer park with a herd of fallow deer.

Sir George Sydenham fought for the king in the Civil War, and his ghost is said to ride down Sydenham Combe on certain nights.

Combe Fisheries lie in the deep valley by Combe Sydenham Farm close to the hall and the ancient deer park. The ponds are fed by springs which in turn feed from the Brendon Hills. They were laid out about the time of the marriage of Sir Francis Drake to Elizabeth Sydenham, and are now a modern trout hatchery. Visitors can feed the fish and have the opportunity to purchase trout, either fresh or smoked on the premises.

On the very edge of Exmoor, where the valley begins to widen out into the Valley of Taunton Dene, is Gaulden Manor. It is nine miles north-west of Taunton off the B3188 near Tolland. Built of local red sandstone this twelfth-century manor house was once the home of the Turbervilles of Bere Regis. Set in pleasant gardens it is open on Thursdays, Sundays and Bank Holidays.

On the coast there is still a lot to see and do. Watchet docks, once busy with iron ore, have recently been given a new lease of life. Many of our small coastal ports declined and silted up when railways took the coastal trade away. At one time almost all goods were carried by sailing barges, which managed to get a surprisingly long way inland. No doubt easier road access to the Midlands since the M5 was built

*West Somerset Railway, restoration work
in progress*

has helped the trade for this small harbour. The church at Watchet is dedicated to St Decuman, a Welsh saint from the Dark Ages. He is supposed to have come ashore from a raft, bringing a cow to provide him with milk. The church and dock is featured in Coleridge's *The Ancient Mariner*, for it was from here that the crew set sail. Watchet museum reflects the history of the port from Saxon days right up to the present day, including both maritime and mining connections.

In the mid-nineteenth century about 30,000 tons of iron ore from the Brendon Hills were being shipped each year. Watchet was an important port in Saxon days. In those violent times it was attacked and burnt by the Danes on at least three occasions. It is the family seat of the Windham family whose memorials can be seen in the church. The family played an im-

portant part in Somerset history. Colonel Francis Windham commanded the garrison of Dunster Castle during the siege of the Civil War. Nearby was the home of Robert Fitzurse, one of the murderers of Thomas a'Becket. The West Somerset Railway passes through the town.

Just over the hill to the west is Old Cleeve. Here are the workshops of John Wood and Son. During the summer months visitors are offered a guided tour of the workshops, seeing the process from the raw skin to the finished products including rugs and slippers.

Blue Anchor has a useful expanse of sands — but is visibly marred by its caravan sites.

Minehead is a blend of old harbour town and modern seaside resort. The holiday camp is well concealed at one end of the town with the eighteen-hole golf course beyond that. At the other end of the town sheltering beneath the towering North Hill, is the old harbour with its lifeboat station. North Hill is a high wooded extension of Exmoor. Just beyond the lifeboat station is the North Nill nature trail, three miles long. A good long, leg-stretching, walk would be to take the Somerset and North Devon Coast Path from its start near the church in Higher Town. It climbs up over North Hill to visit Selworthy Beacon before dropping down to Bassington. Walk back to Allerford, to see the pack horse bridge and the picturesque cottages, and take the path to the picturesque village of Selworthy with its thatched cottages. There is a fine view to Dunkery Beacon from the church at the top of the village. There is also a National Trust information office and shop, during summer months. From here it is possible to climb back up the hill again and wend your way back to Minehead; a round trip of about twelve miles with fine sea views. Both Allerford and Selworthy are noted for their walnut trees.

Back in Minehead, note that the town has a firm sandy beach and an outdoor bathing pool. There is a theatre and boating, riding and fishing. Little England is a model of a typical English country town complete with model railway. Early closing day in the town is Wednesday, although in season many shops remain open for six days.

The heyday of Minehead's harbour was in the seventeenth century when coarse Irish wool was imported for the weavers of Taunton. The town arms show a woolpack and a ship, but when the Taunton clothiers fell on hard times so Minehead's shippers fell with them. There is a short history of shipbuilding round the harbour. The population fell from nearly two thousand to a little over one thousand during the eighteenth century. When the once prolific herring shoals left the Somerset coast, things became worse. The growth in popularity of visiting seaside resorts and romantic scenery came to the rescue and Minehead prospered with that cult.

The West Somerset Railway, which terminates in the town, is the longest privately owned railway in England. The West Somerset Railway was originally sanctioned by an Act of Parliament in 1857 and the line opened in 1862 and reached Minehead in 1874. In 1923 the company became part of the Great Western Railway. British Railways took over in 1948 until 1971 when the line was closed. The present company was formed in 1971 but it was not until 1975 that trains ran. Operating as a viable company it is necessary to use diesel as well as steam. The steam trains operate during summer months as a tourist attraction.

The line has featured many times on films and television; the star locomotive *The Flockton Flyer* is, at the time of writing, having a complete refit. Highlight of the line's tourist attraction is the Pullman Service. In first class Pullman dining cars a full four-course lunch is served as a steam engine hauls the train through the wooded hills and dales of West Somerset.

Minehead is one of the oldest towns in Somerset, and the name is probably of Celtic origin. The church on North Hill is dedicated to St Michael and dates from the fifteenth century; its tower served for many years as a beacon for ships approaching the harbour. The harbour was thought to be one of the safest on the north coast and remained secure in the great hurricane of 1703 which wreaked havoc in many other places.

In 1265 much damage was done in the town by a marauding band of Welshmen before they were defeated by troops from Dunster Castle. From the late nineteenth century up to very recent years the Bristol Channel Paddle Steamers brought in day trippers on outings from Bristol and Newport. The fantastic acceleration, stopping power, and manoeuvrability of the paddle boats made them very suitable for the Bristol Channel ports, especially the winding channel up the Avon to Bristol.

Porlock, with its infamous hill so dreaded by early motorists, has an earlier claim to fame than Minehead. Porlock was attacked in AD 918 by Danish pirates, but the attack was beaten off by the townspeople. In the year AD 1052 the last English king, Harold, landed at Porlock, attacked the town and set it alight. He had been living in exile in Ireland at this time, and his comeback lasted only a few years until 1066. There is a car park near the end of the B3225 at Porlock Weir, where the quaint harbour can be found. Porlock has narrow winding streets and thatched cottages. The parish church dates from the thirteenth century, and has the splendid tomb of Sir John Harrington, who died in 1418.

The ascent of Porlock Hill leads up onto the moor again on the road back to County Gate. Culbone church lays claim to being England's smallest; it is best reached by walking, being just over a mile from Porlock Weir or four miles from County Gate along the Coast Path. Along the A39 between the top of Porlock Hill and County Gate are several parking spaces with attendant viewpoints.

Mention must be made here, before we leave the area, of the Two Moors Way footpath. Starting on the southern edge of Dartmoor and crossing Devon, it arrives on Exmoor by way of West Anstey Common and goes on by Hawkridge and Withypool. The walk crosses the River Barle just below Cow Castle to make a wide swing south and west of Simonsbath. It then heads north over Exe Plain to visit Exe Head, the source of the River Exe, Hoar Oak Tree and the ancient forest boundary. The original oak has been replaced by a young tree. This is a good walk and visits some of the wilder parts of the moor. It is, however, only recommended for experienced walkers.

Selworthy and Exmoor

Montacute House

Lyme Regis

5 South Somerset and West Dorset

The landscape here is rolling hills, higher in the southern half with the Dorset Downs forming that part. The main A30 goes through the northern section, and the A35 near the coast. From Yeovil to Dorchester is the A37 with the A356 joining Dorchester back to Crewkerne. There are plenty of minor roads as well, avoiding the busy main routes. Starting near Milborne Port the area is described in a clockwise direction. Using a base for a few days, say Sherborne or Yeovil, then Beaminster or Bridport for a day or so it is possible, without too much daily travel, to make short forays into the outlying areas.

Being within a couple of miles of Yeovil, Milborne Port and the nearby village of Purse Caundle just get into

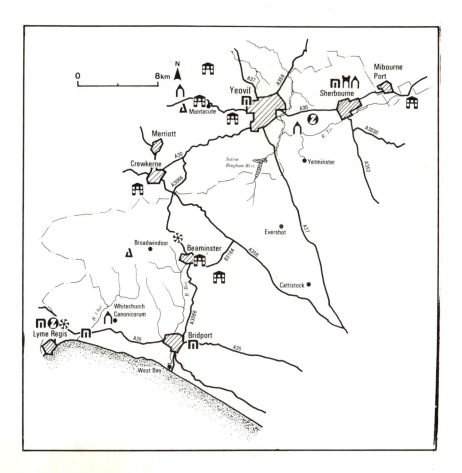

Purse Caundle Manor

this chapter. The beautiful small manor house in Purse Caundle lies close by the stream flowing down and feeding into Sherborne Lake. It is a fifteenth-century house with changes made in Tudor times, and is open to the public on certain days. In the drawing room is an oriel window looking out to the village street. A well in the hall has walls reaching up the stairs, no doubt a device built in case of siege. King John gave the manor and lands to a man who cared for the hounds used when hunting in the nearby Blackmoor Vale. The roof of the hall is original. The church is also fifteenth century and has an embattled tower; the high chancel arch is panelled giving a beautiful effect. In the manor chapel, resting on a desk, is the great bible brought here during the reign of Charles I. It was chained to the lectern for 250 years. It was removed, but after fifty years it was returned to its present resting place.

Milborne Port is a modest town just inside Somerset, formerly more important than it is now. Its church is a mixture of Saxon and Norman. There is an old Guildhall to remind us of its former glory in the days when two members of Parliament were returned by the town.

Sherborne could have a chapter all to itself. The history of the town goes back more than a thousand years, and it claims to be the loveliest town in Dorset. Surrounded by wooded hills with its lake, deer park and quaint old streets to explore it is a gem. Among the modern attractions are an open air swimming pool, tennis, fishing and an eighteen-hole golf course just over a mile north of the town. Half day closing is Wednesdays.

The thousand-year history of Sherborne has seen many famous men. the Saxon Bishop Aldhelm came from Malmesbury to build a church and found the famous school in the eighth

Sherborne, The Old Castle

Places of interest near Sherborne

Purse Caundle Manor House
A fifteenth-century house with the original Great Hall. Period furniture.

Milborne Port
Church, Guildhall.

Sherborne
Tennis, fishing, open-air swimming pool and eighteen-hole golf course. Museum with steam pumps, brass rubbings, agriculture and domestic section and relics from the Civil War. Sherborne Abbey and the Old and New Castles.

Lullingstone Silk Farm
Butterflies in a natural surrounding. Breeding rooms and silk processing.

Trent
Church of St Andrew.

Bradford Abbas
Church of St Mary Virgin.

century. King Alfred may have received part of his education here, and his two brothers, both kings before Alfred, are buried here. Sir Walter Raleigh owned the estate, which was given to him by Queen Elizabeth I. Sir Walter decided that he needed a new house, and that is why Sherborne has two 'castles', the medieval one and the 'new' one. It is here that the story began that every school child knows; Raleigh was sitting on a seat in the garden of his new house smoking when his servant, thinking he was on fire, threw a bucket of water over him.

The sixteenth-century castle passed to the Digby family in 1617 and, still owned by them, is open from June to September every day with additional restricted opening from Easter to June. There is the Lakeside Tea Room for refreshments if you wander from the ruins of the original twelfth-century castle, destroyed by Cromwell, to the

67

new castle. This will have to be by road, as there is no footway between the two. The new castle was enlarged in 1625 and again in 1766 when its gardens were landscaped by 'Capability' Brown. There are twenty acres of lakeside lawns and wooded walks to enjoy. In the castle is a fine collection of pictures with other treasures collected by the Digby family over the last three hundred years. A museum of local history is housed in what was the Abbey gatehouse, open daily from April to October. Exhibits range from brass rubbings and steam pumps to displays showing the history of Sherborne Silk Mill. There are medieval almshouses in the town, and a lovely structure just near the museum which was built as the monks' washing place.

Goathill, a tiny hamlet just over two miles east, has two ghosts — a dog comes down the hill towards Milborne Port and an old lady complete with bonnet and basket has been seen on the road near the Lodge. Sandford Orcas manor to the north of Sherborne, is famous for ghosts, harbouring at least twenty, so it is said!

Two miles from Sherborne just off the A30 Yeovil road, is Compton House, a sixteenth-century manor house. This really is something different, for this is the home of Worldwide Butterflies and Lullingstone Silk Farm. It is open daily from Easter to October and visitors can visit the 'indoor jungle' where the butterflies can be seen flying in as near to natural conditions as it is possible to provide. Butterflies are bred and the breeding houses can be seen, also the process of producing thread from the cocoons to make the unique English silk.

The next village north, Trent, has the interesting church of St Andrew. It has a medieval spire, but much renovation was done in the early 1840s. Of the buildings round the village many date from the fifteenth and sixteenth centuries. Trent also has a ghost, or ghosts. At Trent Barrow, one mile east of the village, there was a deep pit, into which one dark and dirty night plunged a coach, complete with horses and passengers. Since then cries for help and the sound of galloping horses have been heard — on suitably dark nights of course. Lord Fisher of Lambeth lived at Trent Rectory after he retired in 1962 and officiated as curate in the church. He is buried in the churchyard. King Charles II, fleeing from the Battle of Worcester, was hidden at Trent for three weeks by Sir Frances Wyndham in a secret room in the manor house.

One mile south of the A30 is Bradford Abbas; the church of St Mary Virgin is well worth a visit. There is a fifteenth-century panelled roof supported by angels, many carved bench ends and a Jacobean pulpit. The font is over 500 years old with four carved figures supporting the corners. The remains of a preaching cross stand in the churchyard. Land nearby was given in AD 933 by King Alfred to Sherborne Abbey. The monks had a moated farm which is now called Wyke Farm (not open to view).

Yeovil is a moderately sized town set in pleasant countryside. The modern features of the town are an eighteen-hole golf course, bowls and tennis, fishing and an indoor swimming pool. There is an outdoor recreation centre and a cinema. Many of us have heard the name of the town in connection with Westlands, who started manufacturing propeller aircraft and are now world famous for helicopters. This brings Yeovil right up to date, but it was a settlement in Roman times be-

Parish Church, Yeovil

fore being deserted in the Dark Ages. Some claim that the names Yeovil and Ilchester have the same Saxon origin. As the Romans built the road from Ilchester to Dorchester, now the A37, on which Yeovil stands, and the Roman settlement was abandoned per- haps the Saxons mixed them up.

On the A359 at the northern end of the town is the old Hundred Stone, probably marking the former parish, and hundred, boundary. There are good views from here north over the Somerset Plain to the Mendips and

Things to do around Yeovil

Yeovil
Eighteen-hole golf course, tennis, bowls, fishing and an indoor swimming pool. Outdoor recreation centre. Cinema. Borough Museum which has domestic and agricultural exhibits, the Bailward collection of costumes, glass and photographs.

Montacute House
Sixteenth-century house, picnic site and gardens.

Johnson Hall
Varied programme of entertainments.

Stoke sub Hamdon Priory
Fourteenth- and fifteenth-century great hall of chantry house.

Ham Hill
Country park and picnic site from a three-mile walk round the ramparts of the Iron Age hill fort.

Brympton d'Evercy
Manor house, stables, dower house and church. Agricultural museum and the Felix collection of wedding dresses. Extensive grounds including a vineyard and picnic area.

Tintinhull House
Seventeenth/eighteenth-century house with interesting small formal garden.

Fishing
Sutton Bingham Reservoir is stocked with trout.

The approach to Montacute House

70

Glastonbury Tor. In the old days floods in winter often reached from Yeovil to the sea along the River Yeo. The waters have been tamed a little but not entirely — floods came a long way inland in the winter of 1981 when the sea defences at Burnham-on-Sea were breached during a violent westerly gale. Water borne traffic certainly came as far as Ilchester and maybe further, before the railways, and Yeovil received and sent goods by boat via the River Yeo and Bridgwater.

The parish church of St John the Baptist was rebuilt in the fourteenth century from local stone from Ham Stone Quarries. Little remains of the original medieval fittings. The church has been likened to other famous churches, though on a smaller scale, notably the famous St Mary Redcliffe at Bristol, and the nave has been compared with Canterbury Cathedral. It contains a brass lectern dating from 1450. Leather work played an important part in the history of the town; the Wyndham Museum has exhibits of domestic and agricultural interest as well as historical and archaeological exhibits. The museum also features the Bailward collection of costumes as well as displays of glass and photographs.

Four miles west of Yeovil on the A3088 is an area to fill a few days. First is Montacute House, begun in the sixteenth century and completed in 1600 by Sir Edward Phelips, Speaker of the House of Commons under James I. The house has an H-shaped ground plan, and the local Ham Hill stone was used for its construction. It features balustraded parapets and fluted angle columns. Inside is fine seventeenth- and eighteenth-century furniture, and Elizabethan and Jacobean portraits in the Long Gallery. Picnics are permitted in the car park area and teas are available in the tea room from April to September. The estate, which is now a National Trust property, is over three hundred acres and in the gardens are two pavilions which are among the best garden features of the period. The house takes its name from the nearby St Michaels Hill, an ancient earthwork with a folly on the top.

Just over a mile north west is Tintin-

The Memorial, Ham Hill Country Park

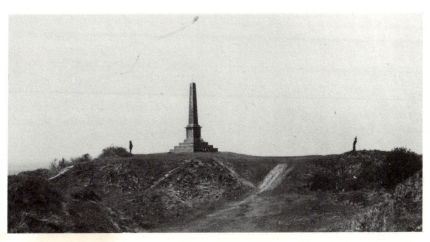

hull House where there is a delightful small garden within the four acres of National Trust property. They were presented to the Trust in 1953 by Mrs P. E. Reiss who was mainly responsible for the gardens as they appear now.

A mile west along the A3088 from Montacute is the village of Stoke sub-Hamdon, where the fourteenth-century Priory is also a National Trust property. The Great Hall is open to the public and was a former residence of the priests of the chantry of St Nicholas. South of the main road is Hamdon Hill, or Ham Hill. Its Iron Age hill fort is one of the largest hilltop enclosures in Britain. The walk round the outer ramparts is nearly three miles and over two hundred acres are enclosed. The walk gives extensive views over the surrounding countryside. It was an important site, placed midway between Cadbury Castle and Castle Neroche near Taunton. The Romans used the hill as a fortified position, as it overlooks the Fosse Way. During the Dark Ages its fate is unknown, but it was used again in Saxon times. There is a war memorial on the hill at the point nearest the main road. Adjoining the main hill is St Michaels Hill, but there is now no sign of the Norman castle that was built there.

The grey-gold stone from the workings of Ham Hill has been used for building locally for literally thousands of years, from the days when the ancient Britons first started to carve out the ramparts up to very recent times. The Roman ramparts and buildings were probably fairly extensive and when the Romans left the site the locals helped themselves to the ready-cut stone from them. When the ready made supplies ran out and serious quarrying began is a little obscure, but through the Middle Ages generations of quarrymen lived in the surrounding villages. The area has now been made into the Ham Hill Country Park, and the land inside the ramparts has been left a maze of hillocks, ravines, terraces and ridges, a delight for children to explore after picnicking. The hill fort can claim to be unique as there is an inn within the ramparts.

Back on the road, towards Yeovil and south of the main A3088, is the village of Brympton. The manor house of Brympton d'Evercy is commended as one of the show places of the region. The Norman house has sixteenth- and seventeenth-century additions. The gardens, stables, church and dower house form a nice grouping. Naturally it is built of Ham stone and the south front was designed by Inigo Jones. The house contains the longest straight staircase in England, there is also a Priest House, an agricultural museum and the Felix collection of historic wedding dresses. Certainly to be counted among the attractions are

---

Places of interest south of Yeovil

Clapton Court
The formal gardens are open including terraces, rose garden, rockery and water garden.

Wayford Manor
Gardens open to the public.

Pilsdon Pen
Ancient hill fort on the highest hill in Dorset. Extensive views.

Powerstock Forest Park
Picnic site and forest trail at Wooton Hill near Wooton Fitzpaine. 1¼ miles of level walking through mature mixed forest.

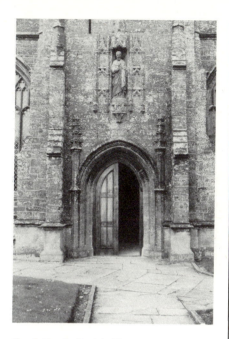

South Porch, Parish Church, Crewkerne

Things to do in Lyme Regis

Philpot Museum
The town's old fire engine and a fine collection of local fossils are among the exhibits.

Marine Aquarium
Exhibition of living local sea and shore creatures, featuring one of the largest fish tanks in Britain.

World Champion Town Crier
This ancient tradition has been maintained for one thousand years in Lyme Regis.

Fishing
Deep sea fishing can be arranged locally. Mackerel fishing trips and fishing from the harbour walls.

Eighteen-Hole Golf Course
On high ground on the outskirts of the town.

Bowls and Sailing
The clubs welcome visitors.

Mini-Golf and Putting Green

Local Bands
Concerts on Marine Parade on Sundays in season.

Regent Cinema and Marine Theatre

the extensive grounds which include a vineyard, the picnic area and a lake.

Southwest from here is Crewkerne. There are some quaint old corners to explore in this ancient market town. The parish church of St Bartholomew is one of the finest of the many fifteenth-century churches in the surrounding area. Crewkerne is a blend of Celtic and Saxon names which gives an idea of the age of the place as a settlement. In Saxon times there was a mint in the town. As in many of the surrounding towns and villages clothiers worked in the town, and serge was made here for the East India Company. Sails used on HMS *Victory* at the Battle of Trafalgar were made here. The records of the year 1830 note that the sailcloth makers of the town made £50,000 from the trade.

Three miles south of Crewkerne on the B3165 is Clapton. The formal gardens of Clapton Court are open to the public and include rockery and water gardens, a rose garden and terraces. There are some rare and unusual trees and shrubs, and a woodland garden. Across the main road lies the village of Wayford and here the gardens of Wayford Manor are also open to the public.

From the junction of the B3165 and B3164, just over a mile east is Pilsdon Pen with its tumuli and hill fort. This is the highest hill in Dorset, 277 m

Lyme Regis

(999 ft). From the top of the hill there are good views all round, especially across Marshwood Vale and down the valley of the River Char towards Charmouth and Lyme Bay, both hidden by the hills. Back on the B3165 one mile southwards from Marshwood is another giant hill fort, Lamberts Castle, nearly half a mile long. It is another National Trust property as is the attendant, but smaller, Coneys Castle just to the south on the minor road.

Another mile along the road is a turning south on a minor road leading to the forest park, forest trail and picnic site at Wootton Hill, part of the Powerstock is over ten miles away to the east, so the forest one time must have quarter miles through beech, larch and mature pine. Though the village of Powerstock is over ten miles away to the east the forest one time must have covered much of the area in between. From here it is only about four miles to Lyme Regis.

There is much to do and to see in and around Lyme Regis. This delightful seaside resort town really can claim to have everything. It is set against a well wooded background with the valley of the River Lym leading back inland to the village of Uplyme. Uplyme covers a large area for a village and is the centre for many walks — it is, for example, possible to walk back to Lyme Regis along the river. The Bridle Path Riding Centre offers tuition and accompanied rides.

The attractions offered by Lyme Regis are extensive and range from quiet gardens to deep sea fishing. If you wish to keep your feet on dry land, it is possible to catch a conger eel from the harbour walls. One of the largest fish tanks in the country can be seen at the Aquarium on Victoria Pier, where there are exhibits of local marine life. The sailing club headquarters are also on Victoria Pier, and races are organized at weekends. The bowling

Things to do around Lyme Regis

Riding Centre, Uplyme
Accompanied rides and tuition.

Barney's Fossil and Country Life Museum, Charmouth

Uplyme Village
A pretty village with delightful walks.

Dorset Coast Path

Golden Gap Estate
National Trust estate of nearly 2,000 acres with fifteen miles of footpaths.

Fossil Hunting
Along the cliffs. Take care, especially after rain.

Morcombelake
Moore's Bakery Biscuit Factory, where visitors can watch the production of Dorset Knob Biscuits.

Whitechurch Canonicorum
Church of St Candida and Holy Cross.

Fishing
Salmon, sea trout, brown trout, on the River Axe. Arrangements for fishing can change so enquire locally at the Lyme Regis information office in Bridge Street.

green on Monmouth Beach is open to the public, there is a mini-golf course and also a putting green in Langmoor Gardens.

During the summer season local bands play on the Marine Parade and there are displays by Morris Men and folk dance societies. The eighteen-hole golf course stands just to the north-east on Timber Hill. Lyme Regis has a champion town crier, and the ancient tradition has been maintained continuously by the town for one thousand years. There is a cinema in Broad Street, and the Marine Theatre offers a variety of entertainment. The Philpot Museum, near the Guildhall, has an interesting collection depicting the town's history. Geology, fossils and lace exhibits make up the exhibitions in the small museum.

A week in August is set aside for Regatta and Carnival, sand sports and sailing races are held and the week finishes with a Grand Carnival.

Historically the town goes back many centuries, the first settlement is recorded in AD 774. For many years the port was one of the most important in England. Medieval records show accounts of ships trading to and from France and later, America. Lyme is recorded in the Domesday Book as having four farms and twenty-six saltmen. In 1284 King Edward I gave the town its charter and 'Regis' was added to its name. Ships from the port took part in the Siege of Calais and the Battle of the Armada. The town was besieged in 1644 during the Civil War by royalist troops commanded by Prince Maurice. The Duke of Monmouth landed near Cobb Quay in 1685 to drum up support for his ill-fated rebellion.

As ships grew larger, Lyme Regis declined as a port. However it was saved by its discovery as a watering place; Jane Austen was just one of the many famous people who came to stay.

The parish church of St Michael the Archangel stands on a site where there is known to have been an earlier church. The present building has twelfth-century features but is mainly sixteenth century. Its peal of eight bells contains five of the original six cast in 1770.

The Dorset Coast Path runs from Lyme Regis to Studland. Almost the entire length is within the Dorset Area of Outstanding Natural Beauty. It crosses grass, downland and limestone cliffs to the sand dunes round Poole Harbour.

Charmouth is only 2½ miles along the coast from Lyme Regis; it is an attractive holiday village with a wide main street. There are plenty of hotels and shops and a secluded stretch of sandy beach leading along to fine shingle. Charmouth was Jane Austen's favourite place.

Many fossils have been found in the cliffs round the Lyme Regis area; in the parish church at Lyme Regis is a window dedicated to Mary Anning, who spent eight years liberating from the rock the first ichthyosaurus known to science, a fish-lizard 30ft long. She received £23 for the fossil, which now rests in the Natural History Museum in London. Mary Anning received a small annuity from the Government and a place in the history books. Charmouth has a small fossil museum, Barney's, incorporating a country life exhibition including a blacksmith's forge and engines used in various farming applications.

Between Lyme Regis and Charmouth is the National Trust land known as Black Ven. It stretches from the coast up to Timber Hill and the golf course.

Town Hall and Museum, Bridport

In all it is forty-nine acres, including twenty-nine acres of cliff.

CLIFF WARNING

Cliffs are interesting and beautiful but they can be dangerous especially after extremes of weather. The cliff may seem safe but be careful. **Heed** all warning notices. **Watch** for unsafe overhangs. **Stay** away from the edge. **Don't** go too close to the cliff base, there may be rockfalls.

East of Charmouth and stretching to Eype Mouth near Bridport is the vast Golden Cap Estate, nearly 2,000 acres of beach, farmland, hill and cliff. It includes five miles of the coast and is served by fifteen miles of footpaths including the Coast Path. Golden Gap is the highest cliff on the south coast of England. Car access is permitted to viewpoints at Chardown and Stonebarrow Hill. There is access to much of the estate but visitors are reminded that most of the land is used as working farms and it is important that crops are not damaged and stock not disturbed. Also, not least, is the preservation of plants and wildlife. The Anchor Inn at Seatown through Chideock, where there is car access to the sea, will provide a lunch stop. Chideock, a very pretty village, has two inns, an hotel and two churches. It held a castle of which nothing remains today except markings in the field. It was destroyed by order of Parliament after the Civil War. There is a Catholic martyr's memorial in Ruins Lane.

North of the A35 two miles from Charmouth is the village of Whitechurch Canonicorum. Here at the church of St Candida and The Holy Cross is the thirteenth-century shrine to the Saint, who is also known as St Wite. Very little is known about her,

Things to do around Bridport

West Bay
Small harbour, eighteen-hole golf course and a boating pool.

Burton Bradstock
Bredy Farm collection of farm implements and tools in a riverside setting.

Bridport
Rope museum, doll collection, art gallery, riverside walk.

Eggardon Hill
Ancient hill site with good views.

Powerstock and West Milton
Churches and riverside walk.

Beaminster
Mapperton House, garden and orangery only.
Parnham House, house, gardens, exhibitions and the John Makepeace furniture workshops, riverside picnic area.
Road tunnel and picnic site north of the town.

Along the A37
Churches at Cattistock, Melbury Sampford and Yetminster.

Penwood Forest Park
Also forest trail, two miles long and steep in places. Approach from West Coker on the A30, Penwood is three miles due south.

Guided Walks
See the notice in the information office window in South Street, Bridport, for a programme of guided walks in the area.

---

but she may have been a Saxon woman killed during the Danish raid. Through the three holes in the front of the tomb pilgrims could put injured limbs for healing. This is one of the few remaining churches in Britain to retain relics of a saint.

Due south of Bridport is West Bay, and sitting on top of East Cliff is an eighteen-hole golf course. There is a pleasant cliff top walk from West Bay to Burton Bradstock with a return route via the bridletrack over North Hill, past Bennett Hill Farm to Bothenhampton and so back to West Bay. An evening stroll along the front at West Bay shows up the lights of Lyme Regis to the west and Portland to the east.

In the nearby village of Burton Bradstock is the Bredy Farm Collection, a collection of old farm tools and machinery in a lovely setting by the River Bride at Bredy Farm.

Back on the main road is Bridport, which is full of history. Among the many old buildings are the handsome Georgian Town Hall and the medieval parish church. The museum and art gallery has collections of geology and natural history. There is a section of items connected with the historic trade of net and rope making. The museum is in South Street and also features a doll collection. Bridport has a carnival week in late August, and a real ale festival runs as a one-day event (enquire locally for details).

The street going south from the Georgian Town Hall has some interesting old houses, including the Priors House dating from the Middle Ages. The town has many buildings from the seventeenth, eighteenth and nineteenth centuries. In the parish church traces of the original thirteenth-century building can be found. Joan of Navarre arrived in Bridport in 1403 on the way to her wedding with Henry IV. King Charles II had a narrow escape from

Cromwell's men in the town and a notice at the corner of the lane leading to Dorchester commemorates the escape route.

Ropes have been made in the town since the thirteenth century. King John ordered ship's cables from Bridport, and ropes from the town used by hangmen were called 'Bridport Daggers'. In the time of Henry VIII an Act of Parliament showed that the Royal Navy had used Bridpot ropes from time immemorial. The most famous son of the town was the Bishop of Salisbury known as Giles of Bridport.

In the information office window is displayed a programme of guided walks in the area. Bridport is one end of the Dorset Downs Walk from Blandford Forum.

From the village of Pymore, just north of Bridport on the minor road from near the Town Hall, it is possible to walk by riverside path to Parnham House, Beaminster. The walk is about 4½ miles, or turn left to Elwell Lodge and return to Pymore on a bridleway over the hill for a round trip of about six miles from Bridport.

Eggardon Hill, five miles east and north of the A35 near Askerwell, is an ancient hill fort 250 m (820 ft) high, giving good views of the surrounding countryside. The ramparts of the defensive earthwork are still 9 m (30 ft) high, and the line of the nearby Roman road to Dorchester is visible. Park in the lane at the foot of the hill, from the top of the hill it is possible to go by bridleway, south-west to Eggardon Farms turning left at each farm to climb back up to the start. The hill was used in the film version of Thomas Hardy's *Far From The Madding Crowd*.

Powerstock village has a notable church, the chancel having a fine Norman arch. On either side of the late

fifteenth-century doorway a figure stands in a niche. It has been suggested that the male figure is King Wenceslas and the female one St Elizabeth, Princess of Hungary. It is believed that King Athelstan had a palace here, the signs of which remain as an earthwork.

Opposite the church is a small lane leading to a bridleway beside the river. It can be followed to West Milton a mile away.

West Milton has a new church, built a century ago to replace the old one. Nothing but the fifteenth-century tower remains of the old church, close to the bridleway from Powerstock. By road it is just up the turning signposted to Leigh (no through road) from the bottom of West Milton village.

Mapperton was the next village north, but during the plague of the seventeenth century the entire population of the village was wiped out. The manor house with its adjoining church is all that remains. The terraced hillside gardens are open from March to October on weekday afternoons. There is a series of stepped ponds in the formal gardens and a seventeenth-century summerhouse, the orangery at one end is modern.

Beaminster is about seven miles north of Bridport on the A3066. The bells of the church play the hymn tune *Hanover* every three hours. The church is mainly fifteenth century with a late Norman font which has a square bowl. Beaminster was Thomas Hardy's 'Emminster' in *Tess of the D'Urbevilles*. Close by the church is a seventeenth-century almshouse, there is a large market place and other interesting buildings. The town was almost destroyed by fire three times, twice in the seventeenth and once in the eighteenth century.

The lane by the church leads on to a footpath south to Parnham House, a shorter walk than that from Bridport. Parnham House is also accessible from the A3066 one mile south of Beaminster. The house dates from the

*Sutton Bingham Reservoir, south of
Yeovil*

Middle Ages and was almost entirely
rebuilt during the reign of King Henry
VIII, being enlarged and embellished in
1910 by John Nash, the great Regency
architect. Parnham was the seat of the
Strode family for some five hundred
years.

Since 1976 it has been the home of
John Makepeace, the world-famous
designer and maker of fine furniture,
and of his furniture-making workshops, while in 1977 the School for
Craftsmen in Wood was also established in this ancient building. Unique
pieces of furniture from the John
Makepeace Workshops are shown in
the main house; the workshops themselves are also open to visitors, who see
the craftsmen at work. Enquiries about
the commissioning of furniture are
always welcome. The School and its
workshops are not open to the public,
nor is student work shown.

A booklet called *Ten Short Walks
Around and Near Beaminster* is avail-
able from the information office at
Bridport at a modest price.

On the A3066 just over a mile north

of the town is the Horn Hill road
tunnel, an unusual feature in our
countryside. Half a mile east from the
tunnel on Buckham Down is a picnic
site which offers good views northward
over the valley of the River Axe. A
bridleway goes north from near the
picnic site down to the river valley.
Turn right and climb back up to
Chapel Marsh, rejoin the road and
walk down to the car park.

Just off the A37 Dorchester to
Yeovil road on the way north are two
interesting churches. The first is at
Cattistock in the valley of the River
Frome. Its handsome church 'would fit
a town'. People used to gather on the
surrounding hills to hear the carillon of
thirty-five bells, the first of its kind in
England. A mystery fire in 1940 damaged the tower and melted the bells,
but the tower was painstakingly rebuilt
in its former style. A former parson
established a pack of hounds and
started the Cattistock Hunt.

Yetminster on the other side of the
A37 has the church of St Andrew
which was originally consecrated in

80

1310 and retains most of the original twelve crosses that marked the consecration. Most of the church is fifteenth century, the original roof and paintings are still retained. Two miles south, just through Leigh, is a mizmaze. Only a mound now remains, but the young men of the village used to recut the paths every year. It was originally raised in prehistoric times, possibly as a ritual site. It was also, supposedly, a witches' meeting place. In the seventeenth century the last witch burned in England was arrested here and executed at Maumbury Rings, Dorchester.

Crossing the A37 again there is a riding establishment at Hillside Saddlery on the road towards Sutton Bingham reservoir.

Penwood Forest Park and forest trail lie about three miles due south of West Coker and the main A30 road. The trail is steep in places, but offers good views to the north and east towards Somerset and the town of Yeovil. The Somerset-Dorset border crosses the top of the hill. The trail has a mixture of old natural woodland and young beech, larch, pine and fir; it passes a badger sett and a pond.

Sutton Bingham reservoir completes the tour of this area. It is due south of Yeovil and can be reached from the A37, being situated in gentle hills with the county boundary crossing the water. This attractive reservoir is well over a mile long and 142 acres in extent. There is a sailing club on the northern bank and the sailing area covers the northern arms and extends a little way down the southern stretch of the water. The waters are stocked with brown and rainbow trout for fly fishing. A pleasant viewing and picnic area is provided with toilets and is fenced off from the water for security. The picnic site faces the sailing club so there are usually boats to watch.

6 Dorset Downs and Bournemouth

Apart from the coastal strip around Poole and Bournemouth, this part of the country seems mostly to have people rushing through. Rushing through to other places, to the coast, to the West Country. This is their misfortune because to pause and look round the area can be very rewarding. To turn off the beaten track and take the byway can reveal treasure. Not only the ancient hill fort, Roman road, or 'big house' and its fine gardens, but also that peace and tranquility that comes from solitude.

Many happy hours may be spent walking along green lanes or hill tracks in this part of the country. Three published walks share parts of this corner of the world. *A Severn to Solent Walk* comes in from Buckhorn Weston to Gillingham and Shaftsbury, it crosses the Downs and goes through Three Legged Cross to the New Forest at Ringwood. *The Wessex Way* comes in from Wiltshire over Bokerly Dyke going south-west to Spetisbury and Wareham Forest. *A Dorset Downs Walk* starts at Blandford Forum and goes by way of Milton Abbas to Bridport. Mostly the tracks are deserted. Walk the Ridgeway or the Pennine Way and you will not lack for

Gillingham, the most northerly town in Dorset

82

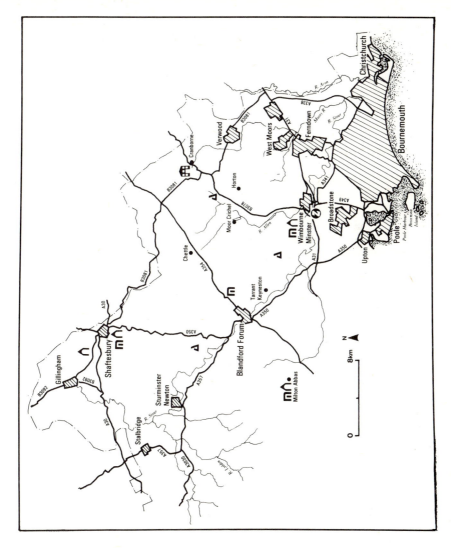

company, walk the Dorset Downs and you will find peace.

Gillingham has the distinction of being the most northerly town in Dorset, an ancient place where much history is recorded. Edmund Ironside overtook the fleeing Danes here. The Confessor was proclaimed king after a *Witenagemot* was held, an Anglo-Saxon national council or parliament. Sir Walter Raleigh once held the post of

Forest Ranger. A grammar school was founded here in 1516 and one ex-headmaster of the school, Robert Frampton, became Bishop of Gloucester. Samuel Pepys, of diary fame, liked his sermon and declared one of them 'the best he had ever heard'. Our ancient kings had a palace here and the remains of the earthwork can still be seen down at the end of Kingscourt Road off the B3081 road to

Shaftsbury.

Just a little way south is Motcombe, a small sleepy village. Outside the church is the stump of an old preaching cross. Preaching crosses were on sites used for worship before a church was built.

South again lies Shaftesbury, a magnificent example of a hill town. Founded by King Alfred who began the abbey, the site was certainly in use before that, as traces over two thousand years old have been found. The abbey was started on the site of a Roman temple and is the burial place of many kings and queens. In those days there were three mints, two hospitals, a thriving market and about a dozen churches. There are seventeenth-century almshouses and an eighteenth-century grammar school.

Now there are four churches. St Peters is the oldest, and its medieval walls look down on the High Street. The crypt, which has now been re stored, was once used as a store by the landlord of the inn which was next door. St Rumbolds has a Norman font. St James has a fine east window and the Victorian Holy Trinity has an effigy which may have come from the abbey.

From Castle Hill the view is southwest to the Vale of Blackmore, and from the terrace walk by the abbey the view is east towards Wiltshire. Gold Hill is an interesting cobbled street.

There was a mayor of Shaftesbury in 1350, and the corporation has a silver seal older than the Spanish Armada. One of the maces in current use dates from 1475.

Once a great procession of all the great nobles of Wessex, led by Archbishop Dunstan, entered Shaftesbury They bore the body of Edward the Martyr, murdered at Corfe Castle by

Things to do in and around Shaftesbury

Shaftesbury
Abbey ruins. Local history museum. Craft and Art Gallery. Medieval church. Gold Hill.

Gillingham
Pleasant small town. Nearby site of King Alfred's Palace.

Motcombe
Village church and preacher's cross.

Stalbridge
Ancient market cross.

Sturminster Newton
Scenic town.

Hambledon Hill
Hill fort and view point.

Shillingstone
Picnic site and walks. Hod Hill and Hambledon Hill, view points.

his stepmother. For a while the young king had been buried at Wareham, then he was brought to a more fitting place for a king to be buried. The nuns guarded the tomb and pilgrims thronged there. The abbey prospered and at its height covered ten acres. Eventually the abbey fell into ruin and was lost. Today the plan of the abbey has been revealed by painstaking excavation during the 1930s. On 22 January 1931, a lead casket was found and claimed as the remains of Edward the Martyr. The remains had been hidden by the nuns at the time of the dissolution and subsequently lost for nearly four hundred years. The abbey ruins may be viewed along with a model of the town as it was at the time of the dissolution. The A30 goes west

Gold Hill, Shaftesbury

from Shaftesbury and it is a lovely
drive to Milborne Port and Sherborne.
South from the crossroads with the
A357 is Stalbridge. It lies in the Vale
of Blackmore, Hardy's 'Vale of Little
Dairies', and although the church is
fifteenth century the tower is Victorian.
The proudest possession of Stalbridge
is the fifteenth-century market cross.
Once a feature of every town, there are
sadly few remaining intact, and the one
at Stalbridge has been restored.

Further east on the A357 is Sturminster Newton. The twin villages of
Sturminster and Newton were divided

by the River Stour and joined by a
bridge, which is over four hundred
years old. Once there were connections
with Glastonbury Abbey, hence the
'minster'. The bridge was built in the
sixteenth century and the church is
fourteenth and fifteenth century. This
was Thomas Hardy's Stour Castle, and
he spent much time here writing his
early books. Most of the houses in the
market square are Georgian. Sturminster Newton can be reached on foot
from the minor road south-east from
Stalbridge. Cross the River Lydden at
Barber Bridge and at Manor Farm

where the road bends southerly keep straight on to join a bridleway which emerges at Newton near the mill.

North from Sturminster Newton on the B3092 is Marnhull. Students of Thomas Hardy novels will know that this was the home of Tess of the D'Urbervilles. Overlooking the Vale of Blackmore the village is scattered around a hill. The church stands near the crossroads, has a handsome pinnacled tower and is mostly fourteenth century. The B3092 leads northwards to join the A30 at East Stour where there is a right turn back to Shaftesbury.

South from Shaftesbury the A350 winds between the hills towards Blandford Forum. Two miles before the town the A357 joins. A west turn at the traffic lights leads to Shillingstone and Child Okeford. Behind Child Okeford lies Hambledon Hill. A good walk goes up the hill to the neolithic camp and hill fort. Here are magnificent views all round; south is another prehistoric hill fort on Hod Hill, inside the ramparts of which is a Roman fort.

Across the river and main road are picnic sites near Ibberton, Okeford Fitzpaine and just south of Shillingstone along a by-road signposted to White Pit. The latter is a small secluded site in young beech and oak. South of the site lie Eastcombe Wood, Shillingstone Hill, Blandford Forest and Bonsley Common. Splendid walks criss-cross through the woods, mostly tracks which are designated as bridleways; they are rather confusing so be careful not to get lost.

Blandford Forum lies to the south of Cranborne Chase and at the eastern end of the Dorset downland. Both the A354 Salisbury to Dorchester and the A350 Poole to Shaftesbury roads pass through the town. Its Georgian appearance is mainly due to a fire which, in the eighteenth century, destroyed the old town.

Blandford is a good town to wander around. There is The Old House built for the German born Dr Sagittary in 1661. Up the hill on the way to Salisbury are the Ryves Almshouses, built in 1682. Alfred Stevens the sculptor was born in the town.

The Bastard brothers, born in Blandford Forum, were responsible for a great many buildings in the surrounding countryside, both houses and churches. At the end of the Market Place is John Bastard's pump and fire monument, it has an inscription part of which thanks Divine Providence 'which raised this town like a Phoenix from its ashes, to its present beautiful and flourishing state'. The monument stands in front of the church of St Peter and St Paul which was built in 1733, also by the Bastard brothers.

Lace was made in the town until 1811. Blandford bone lace was considered by Daniel Defoe to be as fine as any he had seen. Button making was a Dorset cottage industry, and Blandford was no exception. At one time there were four button makers in the Market Place. In 1770, for instance, the inhabitants of Blandford Forum workhouse, three men and eleven women, made fifteen gross of large and small buttons in the month of June.

The Merry Monarch Charles I held a series of reviews all over Dorset and the 700-strong First Battalion Dorset Volunteers assembled at Blandford Forum for military exercises. In 1831 the Dorset Yeomanry were re-enrolled to cope with riots and unruly behaviour of labourers in pursuit of higher wages.

At the very western edge of the town

The Bastard Brother's Fire Monument, Blandford Forum

lie green meadows on the banks of the River Stour. On the opposite bank is the steep wooded slope named 'The Cliff'. At the northern end of this magnificent stand of trees is Bryanston School. Built for Viscount Portman in 1890, it became a school in 1927. The fortunes of the Portman family changed, according to superstition, when they caused the old house to be pulled down to build the new one. In doing so they disturbed the ghost of

'Aunt Charlotte'. It has also been reported that sometimes the lodge gates would open and a phantom coach would go up the drive. Another legend was that if the peacocks left Bryanston the Portmans would soon follow. Soon after the peacocks were sold the third Viscount died. The family sold the house and part of the estate.

Milton Abbas lies six miles south-west, or seven miles if you follow the

Places to visit in and around
Blandford Forum

Milton Abbas
Abbey Church. St Catherine's
Chapel. Rural Life Museum. Milton
Abbey.

Blandford Forum
Georgian market town. Nine-hole
golf course, open-air swimming
pool, bowls, tennis. Badbury Rings,
hill fort with views and walks.
Cranborne Chase. Royal Signals
Museum, Blandford Camp. Chettle
House.

Cranborne
Twelfth-century church. Manor
House Gardens. Lovely village and
a walk.

Knowlton Circles
Bronze Age circle and fourteenth-
century church, roofless but
complete.

Horton Tower
Built about 1750 as an observatory
now almost a ruin.

Dorset Downs Walk. Milton Abbey
was founded in 932 by King Athelstan
as a college of canons; it later became
a Benedictine monastery. A school,
which had about seventy pupils, was
closed towards the end of the eighteenth
century following objections from the
Earl of Dorchester. The school was too
close to his house. Among his
objections he included an assault on
the character of the school's head-
master. It was alleged that he had
allowed the school building to deter-
iorate to the point at which it was

Almshouses, Milton Abbas

*St Catherine's Chapel
and the grass steps
Milton Abbey*

unsafe for the pupils. The poor head-master had evidently used his floor-boards and doors as fuel! His Grace also complained that the boys climbed over his walls to steal fruit and eggs. Thomas Masterman Hardy, Admiral Nelson's Flag Captain, was one of the supposed ring leaders.

The main building is a school now, the building are in better repair, and no doubt the pupils are better behaved. Near the Abbey Church is a map of the old village. The new village was built in 1771 by Lord Dorchester, not just another village moved at the whim of a rich landowner. It took that gentleman twenty years to acquire the houses of the old village as they fell vacant. It took some litigation as well — one owner accused his Lordship of flooding him out. A new church was built for the villagers using stone from the old tithe barn. This was possibly one of the first attempts at building a model village. The 'new' village is very pleasant and caters for tourists by way of a gift shop, art exhibition and rural life museum.

St Catherine's Chapel stands in the woods above the Abbey Church. A flight of grass steps leads up to it and from the chapel there is a splendid view of Milton Abbey church. St Catherine's was originally a Saxon chapel. Its varied career includes re-building by the Normans, and a period as a labourer's cottage before it became a workshop and finally a store. It has been repaired and restored.

North-west of Blandford Forum stretches a beautiful area of gentle wooded hills and valleys, which runs north-westerly up to and across the Wiltshire border. This is Cranborne Chase. A chase was a hunting ground held by a non-royal personage, whereas a forest was a hunting ground held by the crown. Cranborne was a favourite of King John and he was reputed to have favoured a white stag and forbidden anyone else to hunt it.

The chase lies between the A350 and the A354. To the south-east of the A354 is an area of low downland stretching into Ringwood Forest, an area rich in historic remains reaching back into the dimness of time. At the southern end of the B3082 Blandford Forum to Wimborne Minster road is Badbury Rings, a gigantic hill fort dominating the surrounding countryside. There is ample space to park and

stroll round. Bridleways go north-east from each side of the Rings joining near Kings Down Farm, a stroll of nearly two miles. Badbury Rings stands at the site of a Roman crossroads. At the northern end is the Dorset Cursus. The Cursus is two parallel banks about 80 yards apart and over six miles in length. The whole area is rich in archaeological sites, barrows, ditches and tracks abound, and is a fine area for walking. The Roman road running south to Badbury Rings is known as Ackling Dyke. Bokerley Dyke forms part of the Wiltshire border, a huge earthwork across the line of the Roman road. It was built, to fill in a gap between two forested sections, about the fourth century AD to protect north Dorset from invasion.

Two miles east of the Cursus is the small village of Chettle. Close to the church is the elegant mellow brick and stone Chettle House, built between 1710 and 1720 by the Bastard brothers for George Chafin who was then Ranger of Cranborne Chase. House and gardens are open, but conducted

Badbury Rings

tours of the house are available by appointment only.

Along the B3081 to the south-east is Cranborne a lovely village in a superb setting of woods and hills. The twelfth-century church of Saints Mary and Bartholomew has a massive church tower and traces of medieval wall painting. The church was built on the foundations of a monastery, where there was once a Saxon church. Cranborne Manor, behind the church, is a building of grey stone, mostly Tudor with older parts. It is surrounded by lovely walled gardens, laid out by John Tradescant, with lawn and yew hedges. There is a fine beech avenue in front of the house. King Charles I slept at the manor in 1644. Only the gardens are open.

For a walk of just over three miles from just beyond Cranborne church take the road to Cranborne Farm for one mile. Turn north-east on a track and when you meet the next track, at a T junction, turn right and follow it to a minor road and back to Cranborne.

On the B3078 going south towards Wimborne Minster is a Bronze Age henge, a sacred place over 4,000 years old. In this area, so rich in ancient remains, there were many barrows and three henges or circles. Most have been ploughed away but much remains. The church stands in a circle 100 yds in diameter. Roofless for years, the walls are complete, a mixture of sandstone, limestone and flint. It is fourteenth- or fifteenth-century, but of unknown dedication. The village which the church served has completely disappeared.

At the next crossroads south stands Horton Inn. To the south-east is Horton, while above the village is Horton Tower. It can be reached on foot: follow the footpath sign to Horton Heath, then go right through a gate at the head of the road near a house entrance. The brick built tower was built in the mid-eighteenth century for Humphrey Sturt of Horton Manor. It was built as an observatory, but for observing stars or deer is in doubt. Sadly it is falling apart slowly. None of the interior floors remain and it is a very odd looking structure. It is a pleasant walk past the tower into Ferndown Forest, a half mile away, but you will have to retrace your steps.

On down the B3078 is Wimborne Minster, with a history going back to Saxon times. It has a noted lantern tower, a rare chained library and a font 800 years old. A wooden Quarter Jack stands outside still, after centuries, striking the hours. There is the thirteenth-century St Margarets Hospital Chapel. Deans Court gardens are open on Sundays and Thursdays. The Priest's House Museum is a must for visitors. Wimborne is the burial place of Ethelred, the elder brother of Alfred the Great. Alfred himself was here many times and this was the site of his defeat at the hands of the Danes, when they burnt the town and he fled to the Somerset moors to gain his fame by burning the cakes.

To the east along the A31, but to the north of that road, is an area that must be explored. Here lie Holt Heath, Horton Common, Ferndown Forest and Ringwood Forest.

At the eastern end of this tract is Ringwood, over the border in Hampshire, while at the western end is Horton, which was mentioned earlier. Though outside the modern New Forest it is very much the same sort of country, perhaps a little less wild. On Holt Heath you could well imagine you were in the New Forest though the present boundary is twelve miles away.

It was to Holt Lodge that the Duke of Monmouth was taken after his capture on Holt Heath.

In and around Wimborne Minster

Wimborne Minster
Minster. St Margaret's Hospital Chapel, dating from the thirteenth century. Priest's House Museum, Deans Court Gardens, the former Deanery. Merley Tropical Bird Gardens. White Sheet Plantation Picnic Site and walks. Merley Park Riding Stables.

From Wimborne Minster a minor road through Colehill continues on to pass through Broom Hill. Nearly a mile further on is the car park for White Sheet Plantation picnic place, a sheltered site in mature pinewoods. It is quite small, but with attractive walks round about.

To end this chapter is Bournemouth — a seaside town *par excellence*. What can one say about a place that has everything? Seven miles of golden beaches bordered by promenades and sandstone cliffs. The cliffs are broken by deep valleys, the famous 'chines', filled with pine trees. These make pleasant cool walks and give access to the beach. There are two piers: Bournemouth pier has a Pier Theatre which offers traditional entertainment in the summer season; Boscombe pier has an amusement hall at the seaward end. Bournemouth pier has cruise launches and fishing.

There are no less than five cinemas in Bournemouth, and three theatres. The theatres offer traditional farce, a symphony orchestra, opera, musicals, drama, ballet and pantomime. The list of nightclubs seems endless and there are even four casinos.

As befits a town of its size Bournemouth is an excellent shopping centre. Most of the large stores are represented and Westover Road is known as the 'Bond Street' of Bournemouth for the large number of quality shops. Four Victorian arcades enhance the town and Boscombe and Pokesdown are renowned for their many antique shops. Similarly Poole has the Arndale Centre where a wide range of shops, restaurants and coffee bars are gathered together, all under one roof.

The area offers sports of all kinds, including ten-pin bowling, ice skating, and roller skating. The large indoor heated swimming pool has diving facilities and seats for 700 spectators. There are also pools at Poole, Christchurch and Kinson.

Outside tuition and hire facilities for windsurfing are available at Poole, as are facilities for water skiing. It is also possible to have tuition in sailing from one of the many sailing schools around the Poole area. Poole Harbour is almost completely landlocked, so it is comparatively safe. It is sheltered from the west by the Purbeck Hills. It is reputed to be the second largest harbour in the world, and is particularly beautiful with a number of creeks and islands.

Also in Poole Harbour is Brownsea Island. The island is five hundred acres or about three miles round, and has been in the hands of the National Trust since 1962. There is nature reserve administered by the Dorset Naturalist Trust. Boats go to the island from Poole Quay or Sandbanks, and it is open to the public between April and the end of September. There are red squirrels, golden pheasants, a colony of terns and a large heronry. Masses of daffodils are the remains of an attempt at commercial flower growing.

Historically it can go back to the Romans, King Canute, and Edward the Confessor. At one time it belonged to the monks of Cerne Abbey. Four hundred years ago King Henry VIII built a castle to guard the harbour, but little of the original castle remains, and it is now a holiday home. Modern amenities include an information office, a shop and a restaurant. The first Scout camp was organised on the island by Baden Powell in 1907.

Back across to the mainland and back to the delights of Bournemouth. It was a deserted spot until in 1810 one Lewis Tregonwell decided that the area was healthy and had a house built, and so Bournemouth was started.

Of course, at a seaside resort with boats coming in to the pier and a harbour close by there is sea fishing on offer. Poole harbour has a regular boat service, round the island or out to the beaches at Sandbanks. Freshwater fishing is available close by on the River Stour or the Hampshire Avon, which join just behind Hengistbury Head. The Stour we have seen before, but the Avon comes down from Salisbury Plain passing through Salisbury, Fordingbridge and Ringwood.

The usual sports facilities are available, including seven squash centres and twelve tennis clubs. Bournemouth is home to the Hard Court Championships of Great Britain. Also around are eight putting greens, four are nine-hole and four are eighteen-hole. Round and about the Bournemouth area there are no less than eleven golf courses in an eleven mile radius.

For the really energetic Hengistbury Head has a fitness circuit — for the uninitiated it is a sort of minor assault course. Sets of exercises are set up —

Things to do in and around the Bournemouth Area

Eight museums. Bowling, tennis, beaches, fishing. Eleven golf courses. Keep fit course. Cross country track. Boat trips. Three theatres. Four cinemas. Guided town walk. Aquarium. Gardens. Christchurch priory church and twelfth-century castle ruins. Brownsea Island in Poole Harbour, five hundred acres of woods and heath. Rock and Gem Centre, Poole. Poole Pottery. Tourist Information Centre, Westover Road.

---

press ups, sit ups, etc, and one is supposed to jog between them. If that does not tire you out in Meyrick Park on Central Drive there is a $2\frac{1}{2}$-mile cross-country track round a golf course.

Bowling, croquet, pitch and putt, crazy golf, mini golf, cycle speedway, large 6ft x 6ft outdoor chess boards at the end of the pier. Six sport centres, model boat sailing, model car racing circuit. An outdoor model railway offers rides on Bank Holidays and Sunday afternoons and there is also a very large indoor model layout. Four cycle hire establishments operate in the town.

In the area there are no less than eight museums, four in Bournemouth and four in Poole. The Russell-Cotes Art Gallery and Museum features much from outside the area. Sir Merton Russell-Cotes journeyed far and wide, built up an extensive collection and on his death left his home and collections to the people of Bournemouth. The museum includes 200 specimens of rock, as well as sculptures, Buddhist shrines and the town's last remaining Bath chair. Additional attractions at the Russell-

Cotes Gallery and Museum are an aquarium of local freshwater fish and the garden tea rooms.

The Rothesay Museum is housed in what was the Rothesay Hotel, so named after a visit of King Edward VII when he was Prince of Wales (his courtesy title was Duke of Rothesay). Among the exhibits is a collection of over 300 typewriters.

The Casa Magni Shelley Museum is devoted to Percy Bysshe Shelley, the only museum in the world specifically devoted to the poet. It is housed in two rooms at Shelley Park which was once the home of the poet's son.

Bournemouth Transport Department has a collection of vehicles at the Mallard Road Depot. They also operate a mobile museum on a converted double decker bus which presents changing displays throughout the year.

Poole's museums reflect the life and history of the town. The Maritime Museum illustrates the town's association with the sea from prehistoric times until early this century. Scaplens Court Museum illustrates the history and development of Poole, while the Guildhall Museum reflects the civic and social life during the eighteenth and nineteenth centuries. Byngley House is a fine example of a merchant's house depicting the way of life of five hundred years ago.

As a family resort Bournemouth has plenty of facilities for children. There are six childrens' playgrounds, five amusement areas and three childrens' parks. There are paddling pools, an aviary, Noddy trains and trampolines.

There is a team of lively and enthusiastic experts waiting to take you on a conducted walking tour of the town. Their knowledge of the town is prodigious and they have some interesting stories on subjects like the first resident, the smugglers, or just where to go shopping. A modest charge is made; the walks start most days at the Tourist Information Centre, Westover Road, and last for about an hour and a half.

Communication lines for this section comprise three major roads radiating outward from the east. The A30 crosses the northern part going through Shaftesbury. Coming over the downs to Blandford Forum is the A354 on its way from Salisbury to Dorchester. At the end of the M27 is the A31 through the New Forest and Ringwood to Wimborne Minster, while the A338 is a fast route almost to the centre of Bournemouth. A favourite tourist route southwards in summer is the A350, coming down from Wiltshire to Poole.

7 South Dorset

In this chapter there are three main centres from which excursions and outings can be made. Dorchester is the county town of Dorset, to the south is Weymouth, and Wareham is east. Swanage is a little further east, rather cut off from the rest by the Purbeck Hills, with its approaches guarded by the imposing remains of Corfe Castle.

Choosing Dorchester as a centre will allow exploration northwards along the A352. Minterne, two miles north of Cerne Abbas, is the beautiful setting for a large garden in a lovely valley setting beside the River Cerne. The gardens have many varieties of Himalayan and Chinese rhododendrons and Japanese cherry trees. Further north, by about a half mile, is a minor road left going west up to Telegraph Hill. Nearby is a picnic site and from the highest point of the hill a bridleway goes south-east along East Hill. It descends swinging west, to join another track. Turn right and walk up the coombe to enter the wood. The road is beyond the woods, and a turn right returns to the starting point.

Cerne Abbas village lies quietly just off the A352. Ethelmaer, Earl of Cornwall, founded the original abbey in AD 987. The usual growth went with the abbey and what amounted to a small town grew up round it, holding

Stocks outside Cerne Abbas church

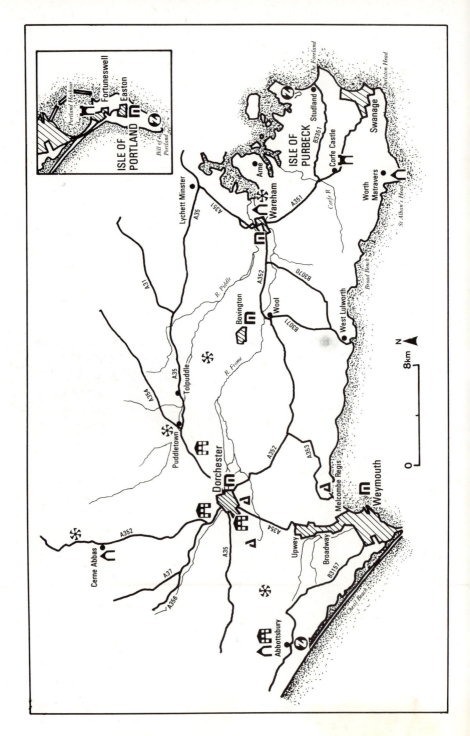

Seafront at Lyme Regis

Maiden Castle, near Dorchester

The New Inn, Cerne Abbas

Cerne Giant

an important place in the lives of the surrounding community.

Quite apart from the fourteen public houses there was a magistrate's court, a malt house and a grain market. Industry included a tannery, as well as the making of gloves, harness and boots. Queen Victoria had a pair of button boots made here.

The last stagecoach passed through Cerne Abbas and the railways never came, they used the next valley instead. The township and its population declined. Now it is a neat and tidy tourist attraction without being vulgar.

Perhaps the virility of the Cerne Abbas Giant prevents the entire decline. The Giant has caused comment, speculation, and no doubt shock, among many people. He is ancient, but whether Roman or older is uncertain. Folklore regards him as a fertility symbol, so he is possibly older than a representation of Hercules dating from AD 191 as has been suggested. Another authority suggests that the Romans merely added the club. A prominent safari park owner and a member of the aristocracy is reputedly proud of siring a daughter thanks to the aid of the Giant. Folklore decrees that women wanting to be sure of bearing children should sit, or sleep, on the Giant's phallus.

The Giant is now fenced off to prevent damage from too many trampling feet, but in any event by far the best view is from the lay-by on the A352, just north of the village, where there is also an information board.

Legend tells of a secret passage from the abbey up to Cat and Chapel Hill. Cat and Chapel may be a corruption of St Catherines Chapel, so perhaps the passage went betwen abbey and chapel.

Just over a mile south of Cerne

Things to do north of Dorchester

Cerne Abbas
Church of St Mary. Remains of the ninth-century Benedictine abbey, fourteenth-century abbey house with fifteenth-century porch. Grounds only open.

Cerne Giant
Ancient hill figure 180 ft long.

Minterne
Gardens two miles north of Cerne Abbas.

Picnic Site
At Telegraph Hill.

Wolfeton House
At Charminster, a fourteenth-century moated manor house. Medieval gatehouse and fine staircase, plaster ceilings and Jacobean oak carvings.

Abbas is Nether Cerne, a tiny hamlet with a manor house and a couple of cottages. The late thirteenth-century church of All Saints is cared for by the Redundant Churches Fund.

Less than a mile south is Godmanstone. Its claim to fame is that its pub is the smallest in England. The story is that Charles II stopped by a smithy and asked for a drink. The blacksmith said he must refuse as he had no licence. Charles granted him a licence on the spot and 'The Smith's Arms' was instantly created.

Just over a mile north of Dorchester is Charminster and Wolfeton House, which was formerly a moated manor dating from the fourteenth century. There is a medieval gatehouse and the main house has a fine staircase and Jacobean oak carvings, although only what was the impressive south-west corner of the house remains. In 1506

Phillip, King of Castile, was a guest here. Travelling from the Netherlands with his wife their ship was driven into Weymouth by a storm. The great house of the district was Wolfeton so it was only natural that this was where they were taken.

Dorchester requires a few days to itself. The Dorset County Museum has collections showing Dorset's natural history, prehistory and geology. There is also the reconstructed study of Thomas Hardy, which contains the largest collection of poems, manuscripts and letters written by Hardy.

Also in the town is the Dorset Military Museum. Hitler's desk is on display, along with a diorama of the Battle of Plassey. Other items of interest tell the story of the Queen's Own Dorset Yeomanry, the Militia Volunteers and the Dorset Regiment. There are displays of uniforms, firearms and medals dating back through history.

Dorchester Old Crown Court is open to the public; it was the scene of the trial of the Tolpuddle Martyrs. They were sentenced here for the 'crime' of forming a Friendly Society, a forerunner of a trades union. Each was sentenced to seven years transportation.

Just south is the gigantic Stone Age hill fort of Maiden Castle, the finest in the country. In 2,000 BC there was a Stone Age village on the site. Later there was an Iron Age village. The Romans commanded by Vespasian captured the fort about AD 44. The discovery in 1937 of a war cemetery with some forty bodies in it disclosed one with a Roman arrowhead embedded in the spine. The Romans laid out Dorchester (*Durnovaria*) and the Roman walls determined the lines of the Walks, the lovely tree lined avenues. These Walks were laid out at the time of Queen Anne when the walls were levelled and the trees planted.

Roman Dorchester covered about 85 acres and recent excavations have discovered remains. Much of the Roman town must lie under the modern town. Many finds are on display in the

Maiden Castle, near Dorchester

Maumbury Rings, Dorchester

museum. The Romans found an ancient stone circle and transformed it into the amphitheatre we know as Maumbury Rings. In medieval England the area was used for jousts, tournaments and revels on May Day. In the Civil War the Parliamentary forces garrisoned it as a fort and lowered the southern bank so that their guns could command the Weymouth road. One of the last events to take place here was the execution of Mary Channing. For poisoning her husband she was strangled and then burned, with an audience of 10,000 people. The amphitheatre is near the traffic lights on the Weymouth road.

Dorchester is a pleasant place to walk around. By the river there is a charming walk. There are pleasant gardens close to playing fields and the avenues measure over a mile. A walk round the town, following the Town Trail, will be most rewarding. A bronze statue of William Barnes, parson and poet, stands by St Peters Church. Another, of Thomas Hardy, stands at the junction of High West Street and The Grove.

St Peters Church is in the centre of the town. It is mainly fifteenth century with a 90 ft tower, and there are some fine features, graceful arcades on each side of the nave, a wagon roof, panelled arches and Jacobean pulpit.

The church of Holy Trinity is Victorian but it is the fifth church to be built on the site. All Saints is in the middle of the town and the tall nineteenth-century spire rises above the surrounding rooftops.

Fordington St George church has splendid views over the surrounding countryside. One of the treasures of the church is a Roman carved stone, one of the earliest known in the county. The inscription is to the memory of a Roman citizen by his wife and children. In the churchyard lie German soldiers, imprisoned here during World War I, guarded by an imposing sculpture of a kneeling German soldier.

Things to do in Dorchester.

Golf
Eighteen-hole course two miles south of town.

Military Museum
Uniforms, firearms and medals from the Dorset regiments.

Old Crown Court
Scene of the trial of the Tolpuddle Martyrs.

Maiden Castle
Enormous prehistoric hill fort, the finest example in Europe.

Maumbury Rings
Stone Age circle, later Roman amphitheatre. Scene in the Middle Ages of bull and bear baiting.

County Museum
Dorset geology, prehistory and natural history. Section devoted to novelist and poet Thomas Hardy.

Town Trail
A 3½-mile trail which takes three hours (plus any time taken to pause at places of interest).

The Hardy Monument,
near Portesham

South-west, on quiet minor roads, there is the oddly shaped Hardy Monument, which has been likened to a factory chimney! It was erected, not to Dorset's man of letters, but to Thomas Masterman Hardy, scholar of Milton Abbas school and later Lord Nelson's flag captain, in whose arms Lord Nelson died. The monument is a 70 ft tall octagonal tower, 700 ft (230 m) up on Black Down; it can be seen by passing ships. This fact would no doubt have pleased the admiral, as he became in the later stages of his naval career. He was born a little further west at Kingston Russell House. Black Down was the site of a beacon, one of the chain set up in 1804 to spread the alarm should the French invade. There are splendid views all round from the top of the Down, although the steps up the monument are now closed. Weymouth, Portland, Chesil Beach and Abbotsbury can all be seen.

A walk of about four miles may be made from here. East from the monument, just below the hill, a bridleway goes south-west to Bronkham Hill. The crest of the ridge is littered with tumuli stretching right along to Corton Down. Here turn south towards the sea. Turn right along the road and soon right again on another bridleway which climbs back up to the starting point.

Portesham is an interesting little village. Like most villages it has an increasing number of modern houses, and bungalows, on the outskirts, but there are many old cottages of mellow grey stone and two hostelries catering for visitors. At the top of the village is a delightful pool fed by a spring. Too grand to be a mere duck pond it has a nesting box set in the middle, designed to be a secure nesting place for ducks or moorhens. A stream chuckles its

way down the main road past the fifteenth-century church. Admiral Hardy lived here as a boy, and again later in his life. He called the village his 'beloved Possum', possibly a corruption of the local dialect.

Two miles west along the B3157 is Abbotsbury, while further along this road to West Bay there is some very dramatic scenery. At Abbotsbury are the remains of a Benedictine abbey with part of the gatehouse and dovecote, and nearby is the thatched Tithe Barn, one of the largest in England. One of the Danes who were raiding in force during the early part of the eleventh century was Cnut (or Canute). Cnut besieged London and in 1017 was recognised as King of England. Along with many of his followers, he became a Christian. One of these followers, Urk, with his wife, Thola, was given land at Abbotsbury and founded the abbey. It survived for five hundred years until the Dissolution when the buildings were demolished. Only part of the nave and the gatehouse now remain. The new owner used much of the stone to build a house, which in turn was demolished during the Civil War.

On a hill just south is St Catherines Chapel. Built in the fourteenth century, its dimensions are only 45 x 15 ft (15 x 5 m). The walls are over a metre thick, as it was built to stand up to the gales blowing in from Lyme Bay.

One mile south of Abbotsbury are the Swannery and Sub-Tropical Gardens. The gardens are in a very sheltered position and contain a very large collection, one estimate is over 7,000 varieties, of sub-tropical plants, trees and shrubs. A separate road leads to the swannery. At one time there were over a thousand birds but now there are about five hundred. They share the

Chesil Beach

Things to do round Weymouth

Abbotsbury
Gardens, swannery, abbey ruins, tithe barn and picnic site.

The Hardy Monument
Set on Black Down.

Preston
Roman temple remains.

Weymouth
Golf, town trail, fishing, museum, gardens and the usual attractions of a seaside resort.

The Dorset Coast Path

Portland
Museum, castles, Portland Bill lighthouse, bird observatory and field centre, viewpoints and walk.

Weymouth, on the sea front

accommodation with many other species, some permanent visitors, others seasonal. The swannery is supposed to have been started by the Abbots of Abbotsbury in Saxon times, but since the time of the Dissolution has been in the care of the Strangeways Estates.

The swans live at the westward end of the Fleet, a lagoon behind Chesil Beach. Chesil is an Old English word for shingle and the beach is a ten-mile long bank of pebbles with the width varying from 200 to 1,000 yards. It is a natural formation with a reputation for dangerous currents, shipwrecks and a variety of cast up objects. It is unique in Europe and was supposedly cast up in one night by a great storm. In the old days smugglers claimed to be able to locate their landfall by the size of the pebbles.

A very tough walk is all the way along the pebbles from Abbotsbury to Portland of ten miles, in summer it is possible to return by bus which runs along the B3157 to Bridport.

Inland is Kingston Russell stone circle, a pleasant round trip walk of just under two miles from the minor road, although the stone circle itself is rather undramatic. Due north and just in the next field are some hut circles which remain as mounds visible on the ground. There must have been a great deal of activity on these downs many years ago for the whole area is rich in tumuli and standing stones.

South of Dorchester lie Weymouth and Portland. Weymouth is a seaside holiday resort and has entertainments of all kinds to offer the visitor. There are facilities for tennis, bowls, golf, riding, yachting and fishing, either coarse on Radipole Lake, which feeds into the harbour, or sea fishing can be arranged. Bathing is possible from the firm sands of the bay or in an indoor heated pool.

Weymouth has been a sea port since

Weymouth, the inner harbour

Corfe Castle

Yachts at Wareham

Roman times, the harbour entrance is well sheltered and vessels may enter or leave at any time regardless of the state of tide, unless they are over 15 ft draught. Now cross-Channel ferries operate from the port to the Channel Islands and Cherbourg. You may see a train running through the town streets on its way to the quay.

There is a town trail which goes through Weymough on both sides of the harbour. It starts at the museum, which houses paintings, prints and photographs giving a history of Weymouth, its local transport, shipping and shipwrecks. In the course of its perambulation it passes Trinity Street, where numbers 2 and 3 have been restored and opened to the public. These seventeenth-century houses are furnished with objects of the period. Further along the trail is the Back Dog Inn in St Mary Street, probably the oldest tavern in the town. Blockhouse Lane is named after the ancient fortifications which once stood nearby. At nearby Preston are the foundations of a small Romano-Celtic temple.

Nothe Gardens, south across the harbour from the town centre, are a delight to stroll in or sit and watch the harbour activity. Sandsfoot Castle, overlooking the harbour mouth, was built by Henry VIII in 1539. Although now only a ruin it was at one time described as a 'right goodlie fortress'. Flowers feature strongly at Weymouth and at the other end of the Esplanade are the Greenhill Gardens, which feature the famous floral clock.

Weymouth is almost always associated with Portland. That is because the Isle of Portland is linked to the mainland at Weymouth by a tenuous thread of road which must cross Ferry Bridge. The land link is by way of Chesil Beach, which of course

carries no road. Portland is one of Britain's natural wonders, a huge mound of stone projecting into the Channel and culminating in the famous Portland Bill with its lighthouse. Stone has been quarried at Portland only fairly recently but there is evidence of

Things to do on Dorset's Coast and Heath

Puddletown
Trades Union Congress martyrs' memorials.

Hardy's Cottage
Higher Brockhampton. (National Trust) The home of Thomas Hardy, the great Wessex novelist. Garden only open, house by appointment with tenant.

Culpeppers Dish
Europe's largest 'swallet' hole.

Clouds Hill
(National Trust) The home of T. E. Lawrence — Lawrence of Arabia.

Bovington Tank Museum
Armoured vehicles from many nations, from 1914 to the present day.

Picnic Sites
On the downs at Puddletown Forest and Affpuddle Heath.

Nature Trail
Affpuddle Heath.

Scenic Coastline
Durdle Door, Lulworth Cove, Kimmeridge Bay.

Smedmore House
House with doll collection, gardens.

Purbeck Hills
Stone quarries, walks.

Roman use; to them it was probably a secure fortress. Verne Citadel, built by convict labour in the 1860s as a fortress at a time when the government was alarmed at the possibility of a French invasion, is now a Borstal Training Centre. Halfway down the east coast is the ruined twelfth-century Rufus Castle. A different sort of castle, built in 1800 by John Penn, the Governor of Portland, is Pennsylvania Castle, which is now an hotel.

Inigo Jones was impressed by Portland stone and used it for the banqueting hall of Whitehall Palace. Later Wren used it for St Pauls. As much as 100,000 tons were quarried in one year as the fashion for Portland stone grew. London University is also built of Portland Stone.

No one could call Portland beautiful but it is interesting. A fine view of Chesil Beach can be seen from the summit, and just east is Portland Harbour enclosing over two thousand acres. The breakwaters took over twenty years to build. It is the home base of the Channel Fleet and also a helicopter air station.

In July the spectacular Navy Days, a two day event, draw thousands of visitors. Portland Castle is now part of the dockyard, but it was built by Henry VIII on the site of a Saxon castle. There is a small museum housed in two cottages which were given to Portland by Dr Marie Stopes. The museum records the history of Portland, the stone industry and the prison service. Down at the southern tip is a car park, a café and Portland Bill lighthouse. There is a footpath going most of the way round the island, giving a walk of about eight miles.

Moving east, the A353 joins the A352 Dorchester to Weymouth road, and to the north of that the A35 goes from Dorchester to Poole and Bournemouth. To the south of the A35 and right on down to the coast there is plenty to do and to see. From the A35 a small diversion south to Higher Bockhampton leads to Hardy's cottage. In this cottage Thomas Hardy, the novelist and poet, was born in 1840. The cottage itself was built by Hardy's grandfather and is in almost original condition. It is a National Trust property and viewing is by written appointment with the tenant, but the garden is open every day. It is approached by a ten minute walk through the woods. Here it was that Hardy wrote *Far from The Madding Crowd* and *Under The Greenwood Tree*.

Hardy's cottage is on the edge of Puddletown Forest. On the other side of the forest, and approached from Puddletown, is a picnic site and forest trail which leads to a good viewpoint over the forest to the Purbeck Hills. The start of the two-mile forest trail is from the picnic site near Beacon Corner at the top of White Hill.

Half a mile east of Puddletown is Athelhampton, a medieval house which has been a family home for over eight hundred years and is one of the finest examples of fifteenth-century domestic architecture in the country. The heraldic glass shows the coats of arms of the families connected with the house, and there is a fine collection of furniture on display. There are large formal gardens balanced by woodland and riverside scenes. The house was built by Sir William Martyn who died in 1503. He was Lord Mayor of London in 1493 at about the time the house building was started. Martyns held the house and estate until 1595 when Nicholas Martyn died, he had four daughters but no son to inherit. Before leaving Puddletown stop in the Square to look at the row of nineteenth-century thatched cottages, a Tudor cottage built in 1573 and the brick-built vicarage, dated 1722. The last Roman Catholic Archbishop of Canterbury, Cardinal Pole, was vicar of St Marys Church for three years. Nicholas Martyn is remembered in the church and there are earlier brasses. There is also a fine stone memorial of a knight and his lady dated about 1300.

Tolpuddle lies another two miles east. Who has not heard of the Tolpuddle Martyrs? Six farm labourers met one morning in 1831 and vowed to form a union to ask for an increase, to ten shillings (fifty pence) a week from the seven shillings (thirty-five pence) wages they then received. They swore an oath of secrecy and for this 'crime' they were sentenced in 1834 to seven years transportation. The outcry at this savage sentence on six hardworking men, two of whom were local lay preachers, forced the government to grant them pardon. However, it took a long time for the pardon to reach Australia, and even then no trouble was taken to find the men. One of them, James Hammett, who was working on a lonely sheep station, read about his pardon four years later when he picked up an old newspaper! This was the first he knew, and but for this chance action he may well have served out his full sentence.

James Hammett is buried in the local churchyard. In 1934 the Trades Union Congress handed over to the National Trust a row of six cottages as a permanent memorial of the events of 1834. The Martyrs' Tree, where the men met in 1831, is also a memorial, as is a tablet on a cottage which was the home of John Standfield another of the martyrs. A gate at the Wesleyan Chapel commemorates the events that shook the world at the time.

South on the minor road from Tolpuddle is Affpuddle, a lovely village on the B3390. The church of St Laurence has a fine tower of grey stone and flint. It is mainly fifteenth century with a thirteenth-century chancel. In the church is a monument bearing the arms of the Lawrence family. The arms, which are quartered with stars and stripes, are said to have been the inspiration for the flag of the United States of America. George Washington's mother was a Lawrence.

Affpuddle Heath lies south of Affpuddle — Hardy used it as his Egdon Heath in his novels. At Affpuddle Cross, one mile south of the village and on the east side of the road, is a picnic site set in pine forest. Three-quarters of a mile east on the minor road is another picnic site, set on heathland and close to Culpepper's Dish which is believed to be the largest natural 'swallet' hole in Europe. This is a large circular pit with attendant smaller ones. They were thought for a long time to have been ancient dwellings. However they are of natural formation and caused by softer parts of the natural chalk subsiding, possibly when sand moved below the surface.

A mile south-east is Clouds Hill and the cottage of T. E. Lawrence (Lawrence of Arabia). He bought the small cottage after renting it for a time when he was serving in the Tank Corps at Bovington. When he left the services in 1935 he lived at the cottage for a short time before his fatal motorcycle accident.

South-east again about a mile is Bovington Camp, an unlovely typical military base, with the heath round about scarred by erosive tracks, although afforestation is being used to repair the damage. For military enthusiasts Bovington is a must, as it is the home of the Royal Armoured Corps Tank Museum. What began as a collection of twenty-six British and French tanks in 1923 has now grown to over 150 tracked and wheeled vehicles. Apart from Britain nine other Commonwealth and foreign nations are represented. The museum shows the development of the armoured vehicle together with armaments, ammunition and engines. There are photographs, models, uniforms and personal mementos. All the regiments have their own regimental museums, but often space prevents large displays, so the Tank Museum houses the armoured vehicles as the general museum of the Royal Armoured Corps.

South again is Wool, where there is a sixteenth-century bridge across the River Frome. Woolbridge Manor, now an hotel, was built in the seventeenth century, and was once the home of the real-life Turbervilles. This was the house where Hardy sent Tess of the D'Urbervilles for her honeymoon. The B3071 south from Wool goes to West Lulworth and on to Lulworth Cove. Both are very busy in the holiday season, but if you can find room West Lulworth has some interesting cottages. Lulworth Cove is nearly circular but opens to the sea through a 400 ft gap in the cliffs. To the east are army ranges, but west is a cliff-top path to Durdle Door and on to Ringsted Bay, five miles away. Here turn inland and join a bridleway back over the Beacons to Daggers Gate and down the road back to the church at West Lulworth.

Kimmeridge Bay is reached by a toll road down to a grass car park. The great black slabs of rock in place of a beach could be a disappointment to some, but the place is a favourite with

Things to do around Wareham and Swanage

Worth Matravers
Old stone quarries. St Aldhems chapel standing on the cliff top.

Swanage
Durlston country park, cliff walks, Great Globe, sandy beach, sea fishing, steam trains at the old station, diving school, lifeboat house.

Purbeck Hills
Ridge walk, Corfe Castle, Blue Pool, where china clay was extracted years ago, now filled and restored as a beauty spot. Pony trekking at Harmans Cross.

Heathland
Walks on Studland Heath. Beach and sand dunes at Studland Bay. Arne nature trail and bird sanctuaries.

Wareham
St Martins on the Wall, ancient church. Old town walls. Trinity Art Gallery. Wareham Forest Trail. Picnic sites at Gore Heath and Coldharbour.

Golf
Eighteen holes at Studland. Nine holes at Wareham.

skin divers. Clavel Tower stands on the east cliff. If was built about 1820 by the Reverend John Richards, who inherited the nearby Smedmore House. It is a 'folly' and unfortunately is unsafe and fenced off. On the other side of the bay, and well concealed, is a 'nodding donkey' oil well. Oil has been extracted here since 1961 at a rate of 100,000 gallons a week. The machinery is painted green to blend in with the background, which it does very well.

Corfe Castle, once a royal prison

Smedmore House was built by Sir William Clavel in 1632; the original parts of the house are still visible, but the west front and entrance are eighteenth century. Inside are examples of fine eighteenth-century plasterwork and an oak staircase. The house is only open on Wednesdays, but it is worth a visit. Much original furniture, collections of Dresden china, a doll collection and the gardens make up the interest at this fine old house.

Inland are the Purbeck Hills and the Isle of Purbeck. Why Isle? Well, consider the geography. The Purbeck Hills reach from Ballard Down, to the north of Swanage, through Corfe Castle almost to Lulworth. East Lulworth is relatively low lying, as a break in the cliff occurs at Arish Mell. North is Luckford Lake, a small stream feeding into the River Frome, which in turn runs into Poole Harbour. In the old days the low lying land would have

been very boggy and difficult to cross in winter, hence the 'island' of Purbeck.

The Purbeck Hills are cut at Corfe Castle and the gap is guarded by Corfe Castle. The village bears the same name. The castle has had a long and violent history. Elfrida, widow of King Edgar, had a hunting lodge at Corfe in 978. King Edgar's son Edward was killed at the gates as he called at his step-mother's house. She later took holy vows and retreated to Wherwell Priory. Her son Ethelred came to the throne, possibly too young, and earned the soubriquet 'The Unready'.

After the Norman Conquest, Corfe became a 'royal' castle; the castle was begun in 1080. Many royal prisoners were held here. One dungeon was only entered by a trapdoor in the roof; presumably no-one left it alive! Twenty-two French knights were left to starve here by King John. Eleanor of

Brittany was a prisoner here, as was King Edward II.

The castle was held for the Crown during the Civil War by Lady Bankes, wife of Sir John. Two sieges were held off and the castle was only taken, eventually, by treachery. In 1646 Parliament voted to have the castle destroyed. Though blasted and mined the castle did not entirely fall and it is still an impressive and awe inspiring sight. The modern road still skirts the foot of the castle mound. The village nestling at the foot of the castle is unspoilt and has the air of a medieval village still.

From Corfe Castle there is a ridge walk in each direction. East to Ballard Point is six miles, with splendid views on a clear day over Poole Harbour. West to Grange Arch, a Victorian 'folly', is just under three miles, down the road and over the fields is Kimmeridge Bay, with a cliff walk back to Swanage for the really energetic.

Swanage is a small seaside resort with a good beach that is very busy in the summer months, a pier from which it is possible to fish, and a harbour from which to organise a sea fishing trip. The Great Globe, carved from a single piece of Portland stone, shows all the countries of the world as they were in Victorian times.

While in the area take the chance to see the stone quarries at Worth Matravers. These great quarries were in production until the mid-1940s. South from Worth Matravers is the twelfth-century St Aldhelms Chapel. Only 25 ft square, it stands on the most southerly point of the Isle of Purbeck, St Aldhelms Head. Durlston Head, south of Swanage, has a country park with access to the cliff walks and views of the lighthouse at Avil Point. Durlston Castle was built in 1890 as a restaurant,

which it still is. It was built by a stone merchant named George Burt, who installed the first pumped water supply at Swanage, and also brought various items of London masonry to enhance the town.

On the northern side of the Purbeck Hills from Swanage lies Studland Bay. This mile-long stretch of well sheltered beach is a great favourite in the summer. Perhaps the most rewarding way to visit Studland is over Ballard Down, or by way of the longer Dorset Coast Path along the cliff edge, passing the Old Harry Rocks. The bridleway over Ballard Down leads directly down to the Anglo-Saxon church which stands on the site of an earlier church which the Danes destroyed in the ninth century. That church had been built about the seventh century on the site of an even earlier building, possibly a pre-Christian temple.

Inland, Studland Heath leads on to Newton, Rempstone, Wytch, Middlebere, Slepe and Arne Heaths, all in the space of some six or seven miles and all on the shores of Poole Harbour. The last one, Arne, has a nature trail and bird sanctuary, and the central portion is criss-crossed by pathways.

We have come round in a circle via the coast and from Arne it is only a short distance into Wareham. Wareham is an ancient town and was once an important sea port. Its fortified site is between the Rivers Frome and Piddle or Trent. The town was founded in 705 by the first Bishop of Sherborne. Its varied history include fortification by the Romans and sacking by the sea-roving Danes. There are three ancient churches, including the small St Martins on the Wall, which has an effigy of Lawrence of Arabia in Arab dress.

The Trinity Art Gallery in South

Street has a changing exhibition of paintings. Part of the old town walls can still be seen and there are some old buildings, although much of the town was destroyed by fire in the late eighteenth century and the majority of buildings date from that period. Wareham now has an east-west bypass saving the town centre from the worst congestion.

No visit to Wareham would be complete without visiting Wareham Forest. There is a picnic site at Gore Heath, on the B3075 two miles north, and another at Coldharbour two miles north-west on a minor road. At the Coldharbour site there is a nature trail of 1½ miles which includes Morden Bog Nature Reserve and a small arboretum. The Wessex Way passes through the forest. This walk joins up the Ridgeway at Avebury in Wiltshire to Swanage. It enters Dorset from Wiltshire over Bokerly Dyke (Chapter 6) so anyone wanting a good long walk could follow the route.

A pleasant path through Wareham Forest

Further Information For Visitors

Barford Park
Spaxton, near Bridgwater.
Tel: Spaxton 269.
Open May to September on
Wednesdays and Thursdays, 2 to 6 pm,
also Easter and Bank Holidays.

Barrington Court
Near Ilminster, two miles north of the
A303 towards Ilchester.
Tel: Ilminster 2242.
House open Wednesdays only
2 to 5.30 pm, mid April to September.
Gardens as for house, plus Sundays,
Mondays and Tuesdays.

Brympton d'Evercy
South-west of Yeovil.
Tel: West Coker 2528.
Open Easter and then May to
September, every day except Thursdays
and Friday, 2 to 6 pm. Cream teas,
estate produce and wines on sale.

Chettle House
Near Blandford Forum.
Tel: 025 889 209
House and gardens open from 10 am to
sunset seven days a week.

Cleeve Abbey
A well preserved small Cistercian
Abbey. Near Watchet just off the coast
road, open daily all year.

Combe Sydenham Hall
Half a mile south of Monksilver on the
B3188 Watchet to Wiveliscombe road.
Tel: Stogumber 284.
Open Tuesdays, Wednesdays, Thursdays and Fridays from end of May to
early October, 12 to 5 pm, hall from
1.30 pm. Home made cold lunches and
teas available from noon. House,
gardens, fisheries, birds of prey care
centre, deer park and corn mill.

Dunster Castle
See under castles.

East Lambrook Manor
Near Ilminster.
Open March to October, Thursdays 2
to 5 pm and weekends 9 am to 5 pm.

Forde Abbey and Gardens
Four miles south of Chard.
Tel: 0460 20231.
House open Sundays and Wednesdays,
2 to 6 pm, May to September, also
Easter Sunday and all Bank Holiday
Mondays. Gardens only 2 to 4.30 pm
on Sundays April to October. The fruit
gardens are open daily 9 am to 7.30 pm
during the picking season. Gift shop,
teas available.

Gaulden Manor
Tolland, near Taunton, Somerset.
Tel: Lydeard St Lawrence 213.
Open Sundays and Thursdays, 2 to
6 pm, also Bank Holidays. Small
historic manor house and gardens.

Hatch Court
South of Taunton just off the A358.
Tel: Hatch Beauchamp 480208.
Open every Thursday 2.30 to 5.30 pm,
July, August and September. Teas
available from 3.30 pm.

Longleat House
Three miles south of Frome between
the A362 and B3092.
Tel: Maiden Bradley 551 or 328.
Open every day except December 25th.
Picnic area, gift shops, cafes, restaurant
and inn.

Lytes Cary
One mile north of the Ilchester bypass
A303. Signposted from the junction of
the A303 and the A37.
Open March to the end of October,
Wednesday and Saturday 2 to 6 pm.

Midelney Manor
Drayton near Langport.
Tel: Langport 251229.
Open Bank Holiday Mondays and
Wednesdays, June to mid-September,
2 to 5.30 pm.

Milton Abbas
Abbey church open daily all year.
Milton Abbey, the house opens during
school holidays.

Montacute House
Four miles west of Yeovil.
Open April to the end of October
every day except Tuesdays, 12.30 to
6 pm or dusk if earlier.
Teas April to September 3 to 5.30 pm.
Shop at the house.

Oakhill Manor
Four miles north of Shepton Mallet.
Tel: Oakhill 840210.
Open daily mid-April to early
November.
Gift shop, refreshment buffet and
picnic area.

Parnham House
Just south of Beaminster on the
A3066.
Tel: Beaminster 862204.
Open from Good Friday to the end of
October on Wednesdays, Sundays and
Bank Holidays, 10 am to 5 pm.
Cream teas, coffee and light refresh-
ments. Picnic area.

Poundisford Park
South of Taunton.
Tel: Blagdon Hill 244.
Open Sunday and Thursday 2 to 6 pm
from May to September. Bank Holiday
Mondays May, Spring and August.
Lunches and cream teas on open days,
in the house or in the garden.

Purse Caundle Manor
Four miles east of Sherborne.
Open April to October, Wednesday,
Thursday and Sunday, 2 to 5 pm.

Sandford Orcas Manor
North of Sherborne.
Open May to September, Sunday 2 to
6 pm, Monday 10 am to 6 pm.

Smedmore House
Near Kimmeridge.
Open on Wednesdays June to early
September, 2.15 to 5.30 pm.

Stoke-Sub-Hamdon Priory
Two miles west of Montacute.
The hall of the chantry house only
open daily 10 am to 6 pm or sunset.

Stourhead
At Stourton on the B3092. Three miles
north-west of Mere on the A303.
Tel: Bourton 840348.
Gardens open all year daily 8 am to
7 pm or sunset if earlier. House open
April, September and October,
Monday, Wednesday, Saturday and
Sunday, 2 to 6 pm, or sunset if earlier;
May to August every day except
Friday, 2 to 6 pm.
Morning coffee, lunch, tea and dinner
available at the Spread Eagle Inn near
the entrance. Tel: Bourton 840587.

Tintinhull House
5 miles north-west of Yeovil.
Open April to September, Wednesday,
Thursday, Saturday and Bank
Holidays, 2 to 6 pm.

Wolfeton House
Charminster.
Tel: Dorchester 63500.
Open early May to end September,
Tuesday, Wednesday Saturday and
bank holidays. Tours by appointment.

CASTLES

Corfe Castle
In the village of Corfe Castle on the
A351 between Wareham and Swanage.
Open daily.

Dunster Castle
Three miles south-east of Minehead in
the village of Dunster.
Tel: Dunster 314.
Open April to end of September daily,
except Friday and Saturday, 11 am to
5 pm. October on Tuesdays,
Wednesdays and Saturdays, 2 to 4 pm.
Closed November to March.
The castle is intact and the interior has
some fine plasterwork ceilings.
Terraced gardens and walks.
National Trust Shop and Information
Centre in the old stables.

Farleigh Castle
On the A366 just east of the junction
with the A36.
Open daily all year.

Nunney Castle
Just off the A361 to the south of
Frome.
Open daily all year from 2 pm.

Portland Castle
Open daily April to September.

Sherborne Castle
Open Easter Saturday to the end of
May on Thursdays, Saturdays, Sundays
and Bank Holidays. From June to
September open daily 2 to 6 pm.

Sherborne Old Castle (ruins)
Open daily all year.

Taunton Castle
Open all year round Monday to
Friday, closed Bank Holidays.

CHURCHES OF INTEREST

Axbridge
Bournemouth Christchurch Priory
Church and twelfth-century castle ruins.
Bradford Abbas Church of St Mary
Virgin.
Brent Knoll
Bridgwater Fourteenth century.
Bruton
Burnham-on-Sea Medieval church.
Cattistock
Cerne Abbas
Chewton Mendip
Cranborne Twelfth-century church.
Crowcombe
Culbone Claims to be England's
smallest.
East Brent
Ilminster Fifteenth-century parish
church.
Kilve
Langport Church and Hanging Chapel,
once part of the town walls.
Luccombe Thatched church.
Melbury Sampford
Milbourne Port Church and Guildhall.
Milton Abbas St Catherines Chapel and
Abbey Church.
Minehead Fisherman's Chapel on the
quay.
Motcombe Village church and
preacher's cross.
Oare Near the Doone Valley, Exmoor.
Powerstock and West Milton Churches
and riverside walk.
Shaftesbury Medieval church.
Sherborne Abbey
Taunton Three ancient churches.
Trent Church of St Andrew.
Wareham St Martins on the wall.
Watchet Fifteenth century.
Wells Cathedral. Also the Bishops
Palace and many medieval and
ecclesiastical buildings.
Whitechurch Canonicorum

Wiborne Minster The Minster, St
Margaret's Chapel dating from the
thirteenth century.
Wincanton
Worth Matravers St Aldhems Chapel.
Yetminster

GARDENS OPEN TO THE PUBLIC

Abbotsbury
West of Abbotsbury village.
Open daily 10am to 5.30pm, mid-
March to mid-October.
Sixteen acres of rare plants and trees.

Ambleside Water Gardens and Aviary
Axbridge.
Tel: Weston-super-Mare 732362.
Open daily, except Monday, 10.30am
to 5.30pm, Sunday from 2pm.

Barrington Court
See houses

Brympton d'Evercy
See houses

Clapton Court
On the B3165 south-west of Crew-
kerne.
Tel: Crewkerne 73220.
Open every day except Saturday,
March to October, 10am to 5pm,
Sundays 2 to 5pm.
Gardens and Plant Centre. Formal and
woodland gardens of ten acres.
Cream teas.

Cranborne Manor
Tel: Cranborne 248.
Open April to October, the first
Saturday and Sunday in the month and
Bank Holidays.

East Lambrook Manor
See houses

Forde Abbey
See houses.

Gaulden Manor
See houses

Hadspen House
Near Castle Cary.
Open Tuesday, Wednesday and Thursday 10am to 5pm and Sundays
2 to 5pm.

Hestercombe Gardens
Cheddon Fitzpaine, near Taunton.
Open Thursdays May to August, also
last Sunday in the months of May,
June and July.
Orangery, rose garden and Dutch
garden.

Mapperton House
Beaminster.
Open 2 to 6pm, Monday to Friday,
early March to end of September.
Orangery, terraced and hillside
gardens, shrubs and trees. Stone fish
ponds and summerhouse.
Tea and soft drinks nearby.

Minterne
Two miles north of Cerne Abbas.
Shrub garden, rhododendrons, azaleas,
magnolias and rare trees.

Montacute House
See houses

Orchardleigh Park
Near Frome.
Limited opening.
Tel: Warminster 216611 for
information.
Terraced gardens, island church,
kitchen garden, good views over lake
and countryside.

Poundisford Park
See houses.

Smedmore
See houses

Stourhead
See houses

Tintinhull House
See houses

Wimborne, Deans Court Gardens
June to September, Thursdays and
Sundays 10am to 6pm.
Wholefood teas.

There are many smaller gardens, a
leaflet is available from:
The National Gardens Scheme,
57 Lower Belgrave Street,
London, SW1 WOLR.

MUSEUMS

Axbridge Museum
In the town centre, known as King
John's Hunting Lodge.
Open daily April to September 2 to
5pm.

**Barney's Fossil and Country Life
Museum**
At Charmouth on the A35.
Tel: Charmouth 336.

Blandford Forum Royal Signals
Museum
Tel: Blandford Forum 52581, ext. 248.
Open all year, Monday to Friday.

Bournemouth
Tel: Bournemouth 291715 for details.
Four museums and four more in
Poole.

Bovington
At Bovington Camp, two miles north
of Wool.
Open Monday to Friday 10am to
12.30pm and 2pm to 4.45pm.Satur-
days, Sundays and Bank Holidays
10.30am to 12.30pm and 2pm to 4pm.
Refreshments available and picnic area.

Bridgwater, Admiral Blake Museum
Open all year, Tuesdays to Saturdays.
Exhibits relating to the history of the
town and the Battle of Sedgemoor.

Bridport Museum and Art Gallery
South Street, Bridport.
Open weekday mornings all year.
From June to September afternoons
Monday, Tuesday, Wednesday and
Friday.

Brympton d'Evercy
Agricultural Museum and the Felix
collection of wedding dresses.
(see under houses).

Castle Cary
Small museum open from April to
October 10am to noon and 2pm to
4.30pm.

Chard
Small museum in a restored
Elizabethan cottage. Open May to
September Monday to Saturday.

Dawlish Wake
Cider Museum and works.
Open all year. Weekdays 9am to 1pm
and 2 to 5.30pm. Saturday 9am to
1pm and 2 to 4.30pm. Sundays 9am to
1pm and Bank Holidays.

Dorchester, County Museum
Open all year, Monday to Saturday.

Dorchester Military Museum
Open all year Monday to Saturday.

Frome
Open March to November,
Wednesdays, Fridays and Saturdays.
Exhibits all relate to local life of
Frome and nearby villages.

**Glastonbury, Somerset Rural Life
Museum and the Lake Village Museum**
Tel: Glastonbury 32954 (information
office) for times.

Hatch Court
The house contains a small Canadian
military museum (see under houses).

Hornsbury Mill
Small museum of bric-a-brac (see under mills).

Ilchester, The Fleet Air Arm Museum
At the Royal Naval Air Station, Yeovilton, Somerset. Two miles east of Ilchester on the B3151.
Tel: Ilchester 840551, ext 521.
Open daily, except December 24th and 25th, from 10am on weekdays and Bank Holidays, 12.30pm on Sundays, closes 5.30pm or dusk whichever is earlier.

Lyme Regis, Philpot Museum
Tel: Lyme Regis 2138.
Exhibits include local fossils and the town's old fire engines.

Poole
Four museums.
Tel: Bournemouth 291715 for details.

Portland
Open mid-May to mid-September, Tuesdays to Fridays, 10am to 1pm and 2 to 5pm. Saturday and Sunday 1 to 5pm. Winter hours as Weymouth.

Shaftesbury, Local History Museum
Open daily Easter to October.

Shepton Mallet
Exhibits from the Mendips.
Ring Wells information office for opening times, Tel: Wells 72552.

Sherborne
Tel: Sherborne 2923 (information office) for times.
Small museum with steam pumps and a domestic section.

Somerset Levels Project Museum
Near Glastonbury.
At the Willows Garden Centre on the minor Westhay-Shapwick road.
Open every day 9am to 6pm.

Street
Open May to October, Monday to Saturday.
Unique shoe museum at Clarks of Street.

Taunton, Castle Museum
The County Museum.
Open Monday to Friday 10am to 5pm.

Taunton, Telecommunications Museum
Open all year on Saturdays.

Watchet
Tel: Minehead 2624 for opening hours.
Small museum reflecting the history of the port.

Wells
Close to the west front of the cathedral.
Tel: Wells 72552 for opening times.

Weymouth, Town Museum
Open Tuesday to Saturday, 10am to 1pm and 2 to 5pm.

Wimborne Minster, Priest's House Museum
Tel: Wimborne 882533.
Open Easter to the end of September, Monday to Friday.

Wookey Hole
Open every day except December 25th. Fairground collection. Madame Tussaud's store room contains, heads, swords, costumes, moulds and other relics.

MILLS

Combe Sydenham Hall
Corn mill and waterwheel (see under houses).

Dawlish Wake
Cider mill in a sixteenth-century barn.

Dunster Castle Mill
See under castles.

Hornsbury Mill

Between Ilminster and Chard on the A358.
Open daily 10.30am to 6pm, Sundays 2 to 7pm.
A restored waterwheel, the mill is set in attractive grounds. Craft shop. Refreshments include morning coffee, midday snacks and cream teas. Small museum of bric-a-brac.

Somerton

Nearby at High Ham.
A thatched windmill dating from 1820.

Wookey Hole

A paper mill with restored equipment (see also museums).

MAJOR ARCHAEOLOGICAL SITES

Badbury Rings

Ancient hill fort. Roman crossroads. On the B3082 between Blandford Forum and Wimborne Minster.

Brent Knoll

Ancient hill site. Near the village of East Brent and Brent Knoll, just off the A370 near Burnham-on-Sea.

Burrow Mump

Ancient hill site, with an unfinished chapel on top. South of Bridgwater on the A361.

Cadbury Castle

Supposed by some to be King Arthur's 'Camelot'. South of the A303 east of Wincanton, near the village of South Cadbury.

Knowlton Circles

Bronze Age henge and ruined church. Just off the B3078 Wimborne Minster to Cranborne road.

Maiden Castle

A giant hill fort well preserved. About two miles south-west of Dorchester.

Maumbury Rings

Prehistoric circle used by the Romans as an amphitheatre and later for 'entertainments' including bear baiting and executions. Near Dorchester.

PLACES OF LITERARY INTEREST

Clouds Hill

Cottage home of Lawrence of Arabia, near Wareham.
Open April to the end of September, Wednesday, Thursday, Friday and Sunday, 2 to 5pm. October to the end of March, Sundays 1 to 4pm.

Coleridge's Cottage

Where S. T. Coleridge wrote *The Ancient Mariner*. At Nether Stowey just south of the A39 Bridgwater to Minehead road. Only the parlour is open, from April to September, daily except Friday and Saturday, from 2 to 5pm.

Doone Valley

Exmoor setting for R. D. Blackmore's *Lorna Doone*.

Hardy's Cottage

Higher Bockhampton, near Dorchester. Home of Thomas Hardy, poet and novelist. Cottage open by written appointment only. Garden open April to the end of October, daily 11am to 6pm.

CRAFT WORKSHOPS

There are so many craft workshops in the area there is insufficient space to list them all. The Council for Small Industries in Rural Areas, 1 The Crescent, Taunton, publish a leaflet listing forty, ranging from basket makers to silverworkers and wine-makers.

STEAM RAILWAYS

East Somerset
Near Frome.
Tel: Cranmore 417.
Open daily April to October 9am to 6pm and at weekends only November to March 9am to 4pm.
Steam train rides, small museum. The largest steam engine *The Black Prince*, in working order. Gift shop and refreshments.

Oakhill Manor
Miniature steam railway rides (see under houses).

Swanage
At the old station near the town centre.

West Somerset Railway
Tel: Minehead 4996.
Open daily April to September.
Operates passenger services from Minehead to Bishops Lydeard near Taunton. This is the largest privately owned passenger railway in Great Britain. Steam trains run in the summer months. A Pullman service operates and a four course lunch is served on a steam hauled train.

VISITOR CENTRES

Fyne Court
Visitor centre for the Quantocks.
Open daily all year.
At Broomfield west of Bridgwater.

Halsway Manor
Folk music and dance centre.

COUNTRY PARKS

Castle Neroche
West of Ilminster, north of the A303.
Country Park. Nature trail and picnic site.

Ham Hill
Country park. Extensive views. West of Yeovil, just off the A3088.

Penwood
To the south of Yeovil, south-west from Sutton Bingham reservoir.
Forest Park and nature trail.

Powerstock
North of Lyme Regis near Wootton Fitzpaine.
Forest Park and forest trail, picnic site.

NATURE RESERVES

Brean Down
Part of Brean Down itself is a nature reserve.

Fynne Court
Visitor centre and nature reserve.

Nettlecombe Court
Brendon Hills.
Thursdays only by appointment.
Field study centre.

Wimbleball Lake
Brendon Hills.
Open all year.

WILDLIFE PARKS

Cricket St Thomas
Just off the A30 between Chard and Crewkerne.
Open all year, summer 10am to 6pm, winter 10am to dusk.
Aviary, gardens, butterfly breeding unit, country life museum, heavy horse centre and farm. Restaurant, picnic area, gift shop.

Longleat House
House open every day except December 25th, safari park open March to October.
Safari park, pets' corner, boat trip to see hippos, sea lions, chimps and gorillas. Picnic area, Victorian kitchens, gardens and orangery.

BIRD GARDENS

Abbotsbury Swannery
Near Weymouth.
Open mid-May to mid-September daily
9.30 am to 4.30 pm.

Brean Tropical Bird Gardens
Bridgwater.
To the north at Stert Flats.
Open daily April until October.
Bird sanctuary and nature reserve.

Portland
Observatory and field centre.

Rode Tropical Bird Gardens
Tel: Frome 830326.
Open every day 10.30 am to 7 pm in
summer and 10.30 am to sunset in
winter.

Studland Heath
Bird sanctuary.

West Hatch
West Hatch, Taunton.
Tel: Hatch Beauchamp 480156.
Open daily 9 am to 4.30 pm.
RSPCA Bird and Animal Sanctuary.
A working sanctuary which houses the
cleansing centre for oil fouled sea
birds. Liable to change as birds and
animals are restored to the wild or
found homes.

Wimborne Minster
Merley Tropical Bird Gardens.
Tel: Bournemouth 740504.
Open daily all year 10.30 am to 6.30 pm
or dusk.

OTHER PLACES OF INTEREST

Abbotsbury Sub-Tropical Gardens
Open mid March to mid October seven
days a week 10 am to 5.30 pm.

Bradford on Tone
Sheppy and Son cider orchard with
small farm and cider museum. On the
A38 between Taunton and Wellington.
Open from 8.30 am until dusk on
weekdays. Sundays from 12 noon to
2 pm Easter to Christmas.

Bridgwater
Old docks and warehouses.

Caractacus Stone
A Roman relic on the B3223 on
Exmoor.

Cerne Abbas
The Giant and remains of a ninth-
century Benedictine Abbey.

Cheddar Caves
Open daily all year, restaurant,
cafeteria, bar.

Culpepper's Dish
On the downs near Briantspuddle.
Europe's largest 'swallet hole'.

Dunkery Beacon
Exmoor's highest point.

Gillingham
Site of King Alfred's palace.

Glastonbury
Abbey ruins, open daily all year.

Golden Gap Estate
Near Lyme Regis.
Nearly two thousand acres of National
Trust property.

Halsway Manor
A residential folk centre and conference centre. Forty-eight weekends of
the year are devoted to folk societies.
Tel: Crowcombe 274.

Isle of Portland
Viewpoints, castles, old prison, naval base and Portland Bill Lighthouse. The lighthouse is open Monday to Saturday, 1 pm to one hour before sunset unless it is foggy.

Landacre Bridge
A fine stone bridge on Exmoor south of the B3223.

Lullington Silk Farm
North of the A30 between Sherborne and Yeovil.
Tel: Yeovil 4608.
Open 10 am to 5 pm daily April to October, including weekends.

Minehead
Lifeboat station and old-world harbour.

Morecombelake Biscuit Factory
At Morecombelake on the A35 Lyme Regis to Bridport road. Open all year Monday to Friday.

Muchelney
The Muchelney Abbey ruins near Langport. Open daily all year.

Poole Rock and Gem Centre
Tel: 677650.

Poole Pottery
Tel: 672866.

Puddletown
Trades Union Congress martyrs' memorial.

Pumping Stations
Westonzoyland
Open Bank Holiday Sundays and Mondays, or the first Sunday in the month, April to September.
Burrowbridge
Open Monday to Friday all year.

Shaftesbury
Gold Hill.

Stone Quarries
On the Purbeck Hills near Swanage and Worth Matravers.

Sturminster Newton
Scenic town.

Swanage
Lifeboat house on Peveril Point. Diving School. Blue Pool, an old china clay pool landscaped.

Tarr Steps
An ancient clapper bridge near Hawk-ridge on Exmoor.

Vineyards
Brympton d'Evercy
(see under houses).
Pilton Manor, Pilton just south of Shepton Mallet.
Open June to September, Wednesdays, Thursdays and Fridays, 12 tp 2.30 pm. Sundays 12 to 6 pm during September. Saturday during July and August 12 to 2.30 pm. Buffet lunches available.

Wareham
Old Town Walls. Trinity Art Gallery.

Watchet Docks
A small working port.

West Bay
Small harbour.

Wookey Hole
Near Wells.
Tel: Wells 72243.
Open all year except Christmas Day from 10 am. Restaurant, cafeteria, picnic area, sovenir shop.

RECOMMENDED WALKS

Brendon Hills
Wimbleball lakeside walks.

Dorset Coast Path

Dorset Downs Walk

Lyme Regis
The Golden Cap Estate has fifteen miles of footpaths.

Minehead
Signposted walks to Dunster and Watchet.

Purbeck Hills
From Swanage to Corfe Castle over Nine Barrow Down.

Quantock Hills
A nine-mile ridge walk from West Quantoxhead.

Severn to Solent Walk

Somerset and North Devon Coast Path

Taunton Deane
Walks in Taunton Deane, a booklet is available from the information office.

Two Moors Way
Northern section over Exmoor.

Wells
Nature trails with descriptive leaflets available from the curator of Wells Museum, Ebbor Gorge, Cheddar Gorge, Somerset Levels.

Wincanton
Leaflet available.

VIEWPOINTS AND SHORT WALKS

Black Down
Near Weymouth, extensive views and short walks from the car park by the Hardy Monument.

Cheddar
Viewpoint after a climb up Jacob's Ladder.

Cow Castle
An ancient earthwork, can be reached from Simonsbath via a two mile riverside bridleway.

Cranborne
Short walk of three miles.

Doone Valley
From Brendon Common on the B3223.

Dooney Valley
A pleasant riverside walk from the hamlet of Malmesmead.

Dunkery Beacon
Exmoor, a short walk from the car park to the highest point of the moor.

Dunster
Town trail.

Eggardon Hill
Ancient hill fort with good views and a short circular walk.

Glastonbury
Walk up to the Tor, splendid views all round from the top.

Ham Hill
Country Park. Three-mile walk round the hill fort ramparts.

Hawkridge
A ridge walk, from Hawkridge church along a road used as a public path, goes to Mounsey Castle.

Landacre Bridge
To Withypool.

Minehead
Parks trail and coast walk to Watchet, seven miles; or to Dunster, three miles.

Pilsdon Pen
Highest hill in Dorset, extensive views from the ancient hill fort.

Polden Hills
Viewpoints from the roadside.

Porlock Weir
Walk to Culbone church.

Shillingstone
Hambledon Hill and Hod Hill viewpoints and picnic site. Nearby walks.

Studland Heath
Short walks on the heath.

West Milton
To Powerstock.

Wimbleball Lake
Brendon Hills.

Wimborne Minster
White Sheet Plantation, short walks.

NATURE TRAILS

Affpuddle Heath
South of the A31 near Tolpuddle.

Arne
Near Wareham.

Castle Neroche
On the Blackdown Hills.

Cloutsham
Three miles through oak woods and
over the moors, Exmoor.

Minehead
North Hill, three miles.

Minehead
Parks walk, $\frac{3}{4}$ mile on level ground
with a tarmac path, following a stream
from Parkhouse Road, near the town
centre, to the western outskirts.

Powerstock Forest Park
Forest trail and picnic site, Wotton
Hill near Wotton Fitzpaine.

Quantocks
Forest trail signposted from Nether
Stowey.

Wareham
Wareham Forest Trail, off the minor
road to Bere Regis.

Wells
Descriptive leaflet available from Wells
Museum for the four trails nearby.

TOWN TRAILS AND GUIDED WALKS

Bournemouth
Guided town walk.

Bridport
See notice in the information office
window for a programme of guided
walks.

Dorchester
Town trail.

Exmoor
Guided walks on Exmoor, details from
the National Park Information Office
at Dulverton.

Weymouth
Town trail.

PICNIC SITES

Affpuddle Heath
Picnic site and nature trail.

Beaminster
Near the road tunnel just off the minor
road.

Brympton d'Evercy
In the grounds of the house.

Castle Neroche
On the Blackdown Hills.

Cold Harbour
Near Wareham.

Dunster Castle
In the park, open as for the castle.

Gore Heath
Near Wareham.

Ham Hill
Site at the Country Park.

Lype Hill
On the Brendon Hills, open all year.

Malmesmead
A tiny hamlet on Exmoor, car park
and picnic site for the Doone Valley,
open all year. An establishment sells
pre-packed picnics in the summer
months.

Montacute House
In the grounds of the house.

Powerstock Forest Park
Site and forest trail near Wotton
Fitzpaine.

Priors Park
Seven miles south of Taunton just off
the B3170.

Puddletown Forest

Quantocks
Picnic site signposted from Nether
Stowey.

Shillingstone
Near Hod Hill.

Telegraph Hill
North-west of Cerne Abbas.

Wimbleball Lake
On the Brendon Hills, open all year.

Wimborne Minster
White Sheet Plantation.

BOATING AND SAILING

Bournemouth and Poole
Boating, sailing, river sailing, rowing,
trips on a luxury ocean going yacht.
The information office will provide
information, Tel: 291715.

Lyme Regis
Motor boats, beach skiffs, sailing,
Tel: 2138 for information.

Minehed
Boating, Tel: 2624 for information.

West Bay
Boating pool.

Weymouth
Rowing boats from the beach and
Radipole Lake. Motor boat trips from
the harbour.
Tel: 03057-72444 ext 7.

FISHING

Bridgwater
Durleigh reservoir.

Bridport
Sea fishing.

Lyme Regis
Sea fishing from the harbour walls or
deep sea fishing. Salmon and brown
trout on the River Axe nearby.

Minehead
Sea fishing can be arranged locally, or
fish from the harbour wall.

Sherborne
River fishing.

Taunton
Chatworth reservoir, in the Brendon
Hills, and Hawkridge reservoir in the
Quantocks.

Weymouth
From the pier and deep sea.

Wimbleball Lake
Brendon Hills, open all year.

Yeovil
Sutton Bingham reservoir, trout.

Further details from:—
Somerset Division
Divisional Fisheries and Recreations
Officer,
P.O. Box 9,
King Square,
Bridgwater, Somerset,
TA6 2EA
Tel: Bridgwater 57333

Dorset
Divisional Fisheries and Recreations
Officer,
2 Nuffield Road,
Poole, Dorset,
BH17 7RL
Tel: Poole 71144

GOLF

Eighteen-hole courses at:

Bournemouth (several courses)

Burnham-on-Sea On the sand dunes, championship standard.

Dorchester Two miles south of the town.

Lyme Regis On High ground near the town.

Minehead Near the sea.

Sherborne

Taunton (two courses)

Wareham, Studland

West Bay, Bridport

Weymouth

Yeovil

Nine-hole courses at:

Blandford Forum

Bournemouth (several courses)

Bridgwater, near Enmore

Shepton Mallet

Wareham

Wells

RIDING AND PONY TREKKING

The following list has been extracted from the British Horse Society's national list.

Beaminster
Colcombe Stables, Broadwinsor,
Beaminster, Dorset.
Tel: Broadwindsor (0308) 68360.
Open all year. Hacking.

Christchurch
Ashtree Riding School, Purewell,
Christchurch, Dorset.
Tel: Christchurch (0202) 482642.
Open all year. Trekking and hacking.

Gillingham
Milton Lodge Riding Stables, Milton
Lodge Hotel, Milton on Stour,
Gillingham, Dorset.
Tel: Gillingham (074 76) 2262.
Open all year. Hacking.

Kilve
The Quantock Riding Centre, Beech
Hangar Farm, Kilve, Nr Bridgwater,
Somerset.
Tel: Holford 374.
Open all year. Trekking and hacking.

Leigh
Leigh Equestrian Centre Limited,
Three Gates, Leigh, Nr Sherborne,
Dorset.
Tel: Holnest 469.
Open all year. Hacking.

Porlock
Porlock Vale Equitation Centre, Por-
lock, Nr Minehead, Somerset.
Tel: Porlock 862338.
Open all year.

Simonsbath
The Gallon House, Simonsbath,
Exmoor, Somerset.
Tel: Exford (064 383) 283.
Open April to October. Hacking.

Timberscombe
Knowle Riding Centre, Timberscombe,
Minehead, Somerset.
Tel: Timberscombe 342.
Open all year. Hacking.

Weymouth
Lanehouse Equitation Centre, Over-
bury Close, Weymouth, Dorset.
Tel: 03057 70177.
Hacking.

Wookey Hole
Ebborlands Farm Riding Centre,
Ebborlands Farm, Wookey Hole, Nr
Wells, Somerset.
Tel: Wells (0749) 72550.
Open April to October. Hacking.

Many others exist, and local tourist
information offices will provide details.

SPORTS CENTRES AND SWIMMING POOLS

Blandford Forum Open air pool.

Bournemouth Keep fit course. Cross
Country Track. Indoor heated pool.
Tel: 291715 for details.

Bridgwater Open air pool.

Burnham-on-Sea Indoor swimming
pool.

Minehead Sports facilities and open air
pool.

Shepton Mallet Indoor pool.

Sherborne Open air pool.

Taunton Indoor pool.

Wellington Indoor pool. Sports centre
and dry ski slope.

Wells Swimming pool.

Weymouth Indoor heated pool. Sauna
solarium and polygym. Tel: 74373.

Yeovil. Indoor pool, outdoor recreation centre.

THEATRES AND CINEMAS

Bournemouth Three theatres and four
cinemas.

Bridgwater Cinema.

Lyme Regis Regent Cinema and
Marine Theatre.

Minehead Theatre.

Shepton Mallet Cinema/theatre.

Taunton Two cinemas, Brewhouse
Theatre.

Wells Cinema and theatre.

Yeovil Cinema and Johnson Hall with
a variety of entertainments.

TOURIST INFORMATION CENTRES

Bournemouth (0202) 291715
Brent Knoll, on the M5 (093472) 466
Bridport (0308) 24901
Burnham-on-Sea (0278) 782377 Ext 44
Cheddar (0934) 742769
Christchurch (0202) 475555
Dorchester (0305) 67992
Dulverton (Exmoor National Park
Centre) (0398) 23665
Lyme Regis (02974) 2138
Minehead (0643) 2624
Poole (02013) 3322
Shaftesbury (0747) 2256
Sherborne (093581) 2923
Swanage (09292) 2885
Taunton (0823) 70479 and 74785
Wellington (082347) 2716

Wells (0749) 72552
Weymouth (03057) 72444 Ext 7 and
(0305) 785747
Wincanton (0963) 32173

USEFUL ADDRESSES AND BUS COMPANIES

Bristol Omnibus Co, (for Somerset)
Berkeley House,
Lawrence Hill,
Bristol.

Hants and Dorset Bus Co,
Bus Station,
Endless Street,
Salisbury.

National Travel (NBC) Ltd,
Victoria Coach Station,
London, SW1W 9TP

The National Trust,
42 Queen Anne's Gate,
London, SW1H 9AS

West Country Tourist Board,
Southernhay East,
Exeter.

Index

Sturt, Humphrey, 91
Sutton Bingham Reservoir, 80-1
Swanage, 108, 110
Sydenham, Elizabeth, 60
Sydenham family, 61

Tarr Steps, 54
Taunton, 41
Taunton Castle, 41-2, 114
Taunton Deane, Vale of, 40
Telecommunications Museum, 41, 43
Thatchcap Windmill, 27, 30
Thynne, Sir John, 11
Tintinhull House, 70, 72, 113
Tolpuddle Martyrs, 107
Tone River, 30
Toplady, Reverend Augustus, 19
Tradescant, John, 91
Tregonwell, Lewis, 93
Trent Barrow, 68
Trent Village, 67-8
Trevilian family, 31
Trull, 42
Turbervilles, of Bere Regis, 61
Two Moors Way, The, 64

Uplyme, 74

Vallis Vale, 11
Vineyards, 13-14
Vivary Park, 44

Wambarrows, 54
Wareham, 84, 95, 108, 110
Wareham Forest, 110
Washford, 59
Washington, George, 107
Watchet, 61-2
Watchet Docks, 61

Wayford Manor, 72-3
Wellington, 40-1, 43
Wellington, Duke of, 40
Wellington Monument, 40, 43
Wells, 14-15
Wenceslas, King, 79
Wessex Way, The, 82
West Bay, 77-8
West Cranmore, 12
West Milton, 79
West Somerset Railway, 43, 61-3
Westlands, 68
Westonzoyland, 30, 33
Westport, 39
Weymouth, 95, 102
Wheddon Cross, 56
Whitechurch Canonicorum, 77
Wick, 46
Widcombe, 40
William The Conqueror, 40
Wimbleball Lake, 57, 60, 119
Wimborne Minster, 91-2
Wincanton, 25-6
Windham, Colonel Francis, 62
Winsford, 54
Withypool, 56
Wolfeton House, 97, 113
Wood, John and Son, 62
Wookey Hole, 16, 18
Wool, 108
Wooton Hill, 74
Worth Matravers, 108, 110
Wydham Museum, 71
Wydham, Sir Francis, 68

Yeo River, 20, 30, 71
Yeovil, 65, 68-70
Yeovilton, 28
Yetminster, 77, 80

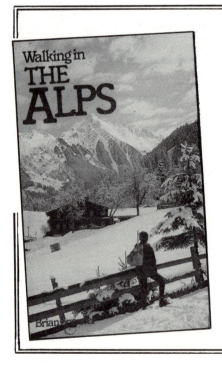

If you are planning a holiday in the Alps and enjoy walking, whether it be a gentle woodland walk or a more demanding high-level route, then *Walking in the Alps* is a must. There are 112 suggested walks each with their own detailed map, based around 16 different tour centres conveniently arranged for a week's holiday in any one area. Places of interest are also highlighted. Illustrated with colour and black and white photographs, the book is 192 pages long and costs £6.95.

Available from:
Moorland Publishing Co Ltd
9-11 Station Street,
Ashbourne, Derbyshire
(Tel: 0334 44486)

Going places?